Praise for *The Man[darin Tree]*

"Pamela and Samantha invoke an ancient magic rooted in Asian alchemy, designed to bridge Eastern and Western cultures to bring greater awareness, understanding, and acceptance of one's Asian heritage. *The Mandarin Tree* is a celebration of life, giving you direct access to greater wealth, abundance, and joy through the Asian American perspective. Through exploring the Asian archetypes, symbology, and rituals presented in this book, one unlocks possibilities for their own grand adventure!"

—GRACE DUONG, creator of *Mystic Mondays Tarot* and host of the *Graced* podcast

"The contribution that *The Mandarin Tree* provides as a resource for Asian American magic and spirituality cannot be understated….Samantha Blossom and Pamela Chen have done a wonderful job blending, balancing, and even reconciling Western and Eastern spiritualities to really define how magic can be Asian American. *The Mandarin Tree* in particular focuses on practices of cultivating wealth, prosperity, and happiness….The practical tips, sourced from ancient wisdom, are inherently valuable and can greatly benefit every single person, regardless of whether they have ancestry from Asia or not."

—DAVID SHI, author of *Spirit Voices*

"A magical and enchanting book that transports readers into a realm of ancient Asian wisdom and modern mystical practices. Samantha and Pamela have masterfully woven together the rich tapestry of Asian culture, infusing it with a contemporary approach to unlock abundance and success in all areas of life.… The book introduces a plethora of mystical tools, rituals, and meditations that empower readers to awaken their inner magic and tap into the limitless potential within themselves. Whether of Asian descent or not, this universal magic welcomes all who seek prosperity and joy."

—GEORGE LIZOS, psychic healer and bestselling author of *Protect Your Light*

"A mystical journey that effortlessly enthralls. Seamlessly interlacing the ancient Asian traditions with modern mysticism, it encapsulates the essence of prosperity in an incredibly enlightening way.…What sets *The Mandarin Tree* apart is its profound approach to wealth. It goes beyond the material and encourages us to embrace prosperity in all its glorious forms—from joy and abundance to the miraculous. This magnificent blend of Asian American magic and mysticism ignites our inner magic, fostering transformation in remarkable ways. Samantha and Pamela serve not merely as authors but as inspirational guides on this captivating quest, helping us unearth the riches that are inherently ours."

—MAT AURYN, bestselling author of *Psychic Witch* and *Mastering Magick*

"Pamela and Samantha share their enchanting experiences with their unique Asian American practice. Through their heartfelt stories, they shed light on the beautiful bond between their dual cultural identities.…I highly recommend *The Mandarin Tree* to anyone seeking to learn and deepen their spiritual journey."

—JEN SANKEY, author and creator of *Stardust Wanderer Tarot*

"*The Mandarin Tree*'s stories and rituals will transport readers to an enchanting world of beloved Chinese deities and guardians. Samantha Blossom and Pamela Chen have managed to capture the endearing personalities and spirits of these archetypes and infuse them into relatable, modern-day practices that honor their heritage and magical traditions. This delightful book highlights the authors' unique Asian American perspectives and ancestral knowledge."

—VICKI ISKANDAR, author of *The Chinese Five Elements Oracle*

The Mandarin Tree

The Mandarin Tree

❋

Manifest Joy,
Luck, and Magic with
Two Asian American Mystics

Pamela Chen
Samantha Blossom

Llewellyn Publications
Woodbury, Minnesota

About the Authors

© Irene Limanto

Pamela Chen is the author of *Enchanted Crystal Magic* and creator of *Witchling Academy Tarot* and *Tarot of the Owls*. She also works as a business, wealth, and money manifesting coach. She helps high-achieving, powerful creatives and visionaries access potentials and opportunities from the quantum field and akashic records through expanding their energetic awareness to infinite possibilities and real magic. When she is not writing or coaching, she loves to cuddle with her chickens, watch Korean drama, and eat spicy Cheeto puffs with avocado. You can follow her magical adventures on Instagram @pamelaunicorn.

© DiamondPhotography—Brianadiamond.com

Samantha Blossom is a manifestation mentor and opulence oracle activating business owners, entrepreneurs, and visionaries to create their most blissed-out life and prosperous universe. Her mission is to teach people to create a life and business that is in alignment with the expression of their soul. She's been in the world of teaching quantum miracles since 2008. She uses a unique blend of Traditional Chinese Medicine, Reiki, BodyTalk, Emotional Freedom Techniques, Accunect, positive psychology, ISBT Bowen Therapy, the Quantum Particle, hypnosis, and several other healing modalities to support her clients in achieving success at the speed of light. In her free time, she loves traveling and visiting healers from around the world. You can tune in to her magical world on Instagram @samanthaloveblossom or visit her website www .SamanthaBlossom.com.

About the Illustrator

© Wen Hsu

Wen Hsu is a Taiwanese-Costa Rican illustrator with many interests and styles, including watercolors, pen and ink, papercuts, and digital. She draws inspiration from her Asian and Meso-american cultural heritage, as well as a wide range of world mythologies she has fallen in love with since she was a child. Wen was awarded with the 16th Noma Concours Grand Prix by the UNESCO/ACCU in Tokyo, Japan, as well as an honorable mention in BIBIANA 2013 (Bratislava, Slovakia) among other international recognitions. Her work has been published in Central America, Argentina, India, South Korea, China, France, Spain, and the US.

First Edition
First Printing, 2024

Book design by Samantha Peterson
Cover design by Shannon McKuhen
Interior Art:
    Chapter illustrations and illustrations on pages 174–179 by Wen Hsu
    Chinese symbols and illustrations on pages 197 & 201 by Llewellyn Art
        Department

Llewellyn Publications is a registered trademark of Llewellyn Worldwide Ltd.

Library of Congress Cataloging-in-Publication Data (Pending)
ISBN: 978-0-7387-7352-0

Llewellyn Worldwide Ltd. does not participate in, endorse, or have any authority or responsibility concerning private business transactions between our authors and the public.
All mail addressed to the author is forwarded but the publisher cannot, unless specifically instructed by the author, give out an address or phone number.
    Any internet references contained in this work are current at publication time, but the publisher cannot guarantee that a specific location will continue to be maintained. Please refer to the publisher's website for links to authors' websites and other sources.

Llewellyn Publications
A Division of Llewellyn Worldwide Ltd.
2143 Wooddale Drive
Woodbury, MN 55125-2989
www.llewellyn.com

Printed in the United States of America

Other Works by Pamela Chen

Crystal Unicorn Tarot
Enchanted Crystal Magic
Tarot of the Owls
Witchling Academy Tarot

Forthcoming Works by Pamela Chen

Caticorn Tarot
Galactic Star Tarot
Steampunk Faerie Tarot

Dedication

So grateful for Elysia Gallo and the Llewellyn family for allowing us to share the magic of our lineages. Big hugs to my Quantum *Jie Jie* (sister) Sam for collaborating with me on this project, and dedicating this to the deities, ancestors, and guides that helped us write this book.

—Pamela

I dedicate this book to my mother and grandmother for passing down their treasures of wisdom and stories to me. I love you both. I am also grateful to Pamela for believing in the creation of this book, and a huge thanks to all of the magical, brave humans on the planet that are ready to step into more power and magic.

—Samantha

Contents

✻

Part Four: Modern Magic

Foreword

Immigrants from Asia brought their Old World folk magic with them to the Americas. The first Buddhist-Taoist temple was built in San Francisco in 1853, dedicated to Guandi, the god of loyalty, brotherhood, and martial arts, offering the divine protection these immigrants needed to defend against the perils of the New World. An ancestor altar with Kuan Yin as the divine patron populates many Asian homes. In Chinatown enclaves to this day, spirit mediums, acupuncturists, and Traditional Chinese Medicine still remain the trusted curative approaches for health. Fortune-telling with divination stalks, moon blocks, and Ba-Zi astrology are annual traditions for forecasting the year ahead. Feng shui must be accounted for in home buying, interior decor, and burials. So begins the first introduction of Asian magic and mysticism to the Americas.

The children of these immigrants then reconcile Old World folk magic with the modern day. Now a new generation of Asian Americans like Pamela and Samantha are leading a syncretized practice that integrates cultural artifacts from our ancestral heritage with eclectic pagan and New Age spirituality. *The Mandarin*

Tree is a transformative thesis of that contemporary Taiwanese American spiritual experience, one dialed in to center the achievement of personal success and well-being.

Whether it is the Lunar New Year or the Mid-Autumn Harvest Moon, a gift of mandarin oranges is a gift of blessings for prosperity and good fortune. If the peach tree of Taoist mysticism is the axis mundi—the world pillar—bearing the fruit of immortality, then the mandarin is a tree of paradise, bearing the fruit of happiness and contentment. In this fresh, practical guide to Asian American magic, Pamela and Samantha share ritual practices that invite you to cross the threshold and begin a journey of perpetual, sustainable prosperity. That journey is marked by a vision of the sacred mandarin tree.

In feng shui, planting a mandarin tree in the southeast or eastern bounds of your home will bring year-round financial prosperity. Planted in the northeast, mastery of specialized arts and academic excellence will flourish. In-home ornamental money trees serve as a form of sympathetic magic, whereby their resemblance to a mandarin tree activates a correspondence to ever-growing perennial bounty.

The principle of correspondences is fundamental to Asian folk traditions. That principle of correspondences is the undercurrent of what Pamela and Samantha share. The magic of words means that homonyms are powerful nexus points, and so, per Old World traditions, eating fish *yú* 魚 ensures blessings of *yú* 余, abundance and plenitude. The mandarin orange *jú* 桔 can magically manifest *jí* 吉, which means to be auspicious and lucky.

Both the mandarin and the word for amplifying joy and luck share the same root radicals "口" (*kǒu*, a gateway or portal) and "士" (*shì*, one possessing specialized knowledge and skill), further strengthening the magnetic tether between the two. Incidentally, the portal and the Skilled One are emblematic of what *The Mandarin Tree* embodies. Likewise, the sacred activation codes this book teaches are premised on that traditional magic of words and their magnetic tethers to intentions.

This book also presents basic *Wu Xing* Five Elements philosophy that anyone can integrate into modern spell-crafting. Wood, Fire, Earth, Metal, and Water govern the astrological influences of the five planets. In turn, Jupiter, Mars, Saturn, Venus, and Mercury correspond with the five points that square the circle, connecting Earth (the square) and Heaven (the circle). Those five points that square the circle—east, south, center, west, and north—can be controlled by the five fingers at the palm of the mystic's hand, which in turn reveal all there is to know about the five stages of human life: birth, childhood, adolescence, adulthood, and death.

What I love about *The Mandarin Tree* is its deeply personal approach to merging popular metaphysical practices of the West with popular metaphysical practices of the East, and how it augments inherited cultural traditions with newly discovered spiritual movements. It is fully and truly "Asian American" in the ways it hyphenates different modalities of magic, such as utilizing tarot cards for invoking Kuan Yin and the Laughing Buddha, or working with crystals and gemstones as feng shui cures.

Pamela and I first connected in 2018 when she released the *Crystal Unicorn Tarot* and later through her *Witchling Academy Tarot* and *Tarot of the Owls*. We ran in the same social circles and soon we had the chance to meet in person. She is as vibrant and effervescent in person as you would imagine, sparkling and kind. You would never know the ways she has had to "endure bitterness," or *chi ku* 吃苦 as we would say in Mandarin. Pamela's indomitable spirit has kept her a dreamer, no matter the harsh realities she has faced. True strength and resilience are most evident in those who do not let adversity weather away their compassion.

Samantha and I share a similar family history of descending from village healers and spirit mediums in southern Taiwan. Our grandparents and great-grandparents approached medicine in a way that was part shamanistic faith healing and part folk knowledge of herbs. Samantha inherited that life's mission to heal, bearing the intuitive knowledge that at its root, illness begins as a rupture in the spirit, and therefore energy healing is often the key line of defense. She is a mystic whose holistic approach draws from acupuncture, Traditional Chinese Medicine (TCM), qigong, hypnotherapy, and Reiki, informed by a degree in biochemistry. Samantha now facilitates transformative spiritual journeys by bridging the old ways with the new, augmenting TCM theory with twenty-first century propositions on quantum magic.

Without further ado, let us cross the prosperity portal of the mandarin tree. Beyond the threshold, we will connect with mythical archetypes such as the tiger spirit, the animal messenger of the Queen Mother of the West, a primordial goddess venerated by mystics and healers, oft channeled by the *dang gi* like Samantha's great-grandfather. Work with the dragon spirit to bring in blessings of great power, prestige, and realized talent. The three-legged *Jin Chan* money frog is one of my personal favorites for attracting a steady flow of income, and to ensure that my pursuits are continually profitable. May Pamela and Samantha's unique, deeply personal approaches to Asian American magic inspire your own extraordinary multicultural path to awakening.

—BENEBELL WEN

AUTHOR OF *THE TAO OF CRAFT* AND *I CHING, THE ORACLE*

Preface
The Mandarin Tree
Prosperity Portal

Mandarin oranges are a traditional symbol of luck, prosperity, and abundance in some Asian cultures. They are an important symbol of Chinese New Year and are said to bring happiness and good fortune to our lives. The color of this auspicious fruit is also said to symbolize gold. By opening this book, perhaps you were looking for a little more joy, luck, and magic in your life. Well, you are in the right place. Before you read any further, we would like to help you access the Mandarin Tree Prosperity Portal so that you can start tapping into its high-vibe, good-fortune frequency. Just relax, follow the exercise below, and step into abundance magic now.

Begin by standing up. Focus on rooting yourself into the ground. Imagine your feet turning into the roots of a mandarin tree. Feel your roots go deep, deep into the earth. Flowing up your body is your powerful and sturdy trunk. Spread your arms and fingers out; they are the branches and leaves of your tree. Sway to your inner music of abundance as you imagine little mandarin oranges growing on your branches. As your heart opens, you feel like anything is possible for you, and you feel good fortune running through your entire body. Feel how good it feels to be this mandarin tree, welcoming all the prosperity and beautiful experiences that are growing in your life.

When you are ready, bring your awareness back to your present surroundings. You have now unlocked your inner mandarin tree magic, stepped into the prosperity portal, and are prepped for the rest of this book. Welcome.

Introduction

The magic of the East has influenced Asian culture for millennia, and it is now being seen and heard all over the world. Many modern healing modalities and magical practices include energies and rituals that originated in ancient Asian arts such as acupuncture, Reiki, and feng shui. It is our mission to spread these sacred practices and enchantments, because we believe that everyone who engages with our magical Asian culture will benefit greatly from all that it has to offer.

Just so you know, you don't have to be Asian to benefit from this book. It doesn't matter if you are of Asian descent in this lifetime or not—this magic, like all magic, is universal. If you believe, as we do, that we are all one energy, then anyone is allowed access to Asian magic, as well as other kinds of magic. Of course, it is important to always treat practices with respect and integrity.

What we share in this book is not your typical Asian American folk magic. We are modern mystics, and in this book we will share unique transmissions and downloads we received from our guides. We are excited to introduce you to this realm filled with mythical deities, golden ancestors, and powerful animal guides.

Working with the divine magic in this book will show you how to create a life surrounded by what you most desire. The magical practices we will be sharing are a mixture of our Asian American cultures; while we still have connections to our traditional Taiwanese and Chinese magic, each of us has expanded in our personal practice, and we incorporate many modern ways to work with these ancient energies. Our life experiences are influenced by both the East and the West, and our magic alchemized into something that supported us in the current moment. In *The Mandarin Tree*, you will be diving into enchantments that trace back to our childhoods as well as the magical lessons we have learned and incorporated into our own lives. Before we share this magic with you, we want to discuss our life experiences that were the inspiration behind this epic book.

The Story of Two Asian American Mystics

Samantha grew up in a small town close to Portland, Oregon, called Vancouver, Washington, and from the time she was a baby girl, she spent her summers in Taipei, Taiwan. Living in two countries opened her mind to various ways of living and perspectives on life. From a young age, she was surrounded by Buddhist monks, sages, famous Chinese medicine practitioners, and shamanic healers that helped shape her awareness of miraculous, spontaneous healings as the norm. While in Taiwan, she often found herself at elegant dinner parties where elaborate displays of mandarin oranges were served, and she would wonder if there was any secret magical meaning to this tradition.

Later, Samantha moved to California and studied biochemistry at Whittier College, where she also did all of her premed studies. After college she moved to Shanghai, China, where she studied Traditional Chinese Medicine. Due to some of the pressures of living in a foreign country and being so far away from friends and family, Samantha developed a severe form of bronchitis where she coughed blood for over three months. In hopes of healing herself, she went to several acupuncturists, herbal medicine practitioners, and Western medical practitioners. It wasn't until she found energy medicine and quantum healing that her symptoms subsided overnight, and she was able to breathe and sleep deeply again. After her body miraculously healed through energy work, she decided she needed to study energy medicine from as many teachers as she could find. She went on to study with teachers from Japan, Singapore, the UK, Ireland, Hong Kong, Taiwan, and several parts of the US. Through her darkest moments, her connection to magic was born.

Pamela was born in Taiwan and moved to Hawaii when she was around age five. Hawaii is a magical place to live in, and Pamela loved growing up on the island of Oahu. At the first house she lived in, there was a mandarin orange tree she ate from all the time. She remembers a Feng Shui Master coming by and saying that this tree would bring good fortune to the home.

At the age of sixteen, Pamela moved out, and she struggled with being poor and out of alignment with her purpose for most of her teenage years. The best decision she ever made was moving to Las Vegas, Nevada, at the age of twenty. It was at this time she was guided to her first psychic mentor and Reiki teacher. Since that time, Pamela has become certified in many healing modalities, tools of manifestation, money magic, online coaching, and so much more. After years of practicing magic—the very same magic we are sharing with you in this book—Pamela was able to quit her four jobs, create a six-figure online business, and sign nine publishing contracts with successful companies. All of this was accomplished by someone who didn't go to college and for whom English is a second language. Pamela is committed to living an extraordinary life and to sharing this same magic with others.

The way that Samantha and Pamela were introduced to each other was also very magical. At the time, Pamela was looking for a money coach for a mastermind program she was hosting, and a friend of a friend suggested Samantha. Once Pamela looked at her Instagram page, she knew right away that Samantha was someone she wanted to collaborate with, or at least get to know as a friend. Luckily, Samantha said yes, and a beautiful friendship and working relationship began.

Whenever Pamela and Samantha messaged each other, it always put them both in great moods, and they found they could talk to one another so easily. They began having in-depth conversations about magic and discovered that they were both studying the mystical frequencies of wealth, abundance, and magic. Not only that, but they had many energetic practices in common.

Samantha and Pamela also bonded over their similar cultures and backgrounds. Little did they know that while young Samantha was in Taiwan asking her mom why they always had mandarin oranges after every dinner, little Pamela was picking mandarin oranges from the tree outside her home thousands of miles away. Now, Samantha is Pamela's *Jie Jie*, which means older sister, though not by much. This is considered a title of respect in Chinese culture. Pamela is *Mei Mei*, which means little sister.

For an entire year, Samantha and Pamela committed to working their magic together, and they began to manifest even more opportunities and miracles in their lives. One random day, they started talking about how the magic they were practicing—which was based on so many of the Asian deities and practices they were both familiar with—should be a program or even a book. Pamela, who tends to both make decisions and act quickly, was so excited and believed in this idea so much, she created an entire book map in one day. Within a couple of months, the book proposal was submitted, and *The Mandarin Tree* was born!

A Map to the Mandarin Tree

We hope that this book empowers you to explore your own magic and the many mysteries of modern Asian American magic. The practices in this book are the same foundational practices we use in our own lives to cultivate good fortune and success, as well as to navigate life's daily challenges. It is our greatest wish to bring even more joy, luck, and magic into your everyday life through these simple, intentional practices inspired by Asian culture.

If you are noticing that this book focuses a lot on money, wealth, and good fortune, this is because our culture believes that is the most significant part of our lives. If we can create a life of abundance, especially generational wealth, then our families will be taken care of. It is even more important to manifest and pray for abundance than it is to pray for loving relationships, because it is believed that if you are wealthy, then you will be able to find a good partner. As this is the belief within our culture, it is deeply embedded in our magical practices. This book is not just about manifesting more money, however: the philosophies in *The Mandarin Tree* are about wealth in all areas of life.

The magic of riches lives inside of you—it always has. When you learn to tap into enchanted wisdom and modern Asian American prosperity magic, additional intuitive awareness will awaken and unfold within you. Like an ever-blossoming rose, the more deeply you dive into these mysterious tools, the more your own magic will reveal itself to you. As you explore the different chapters in this book, and the playful archetypes and characters that will be introduced, you will activate, awaken, and bring to life energy that already resides within you. Bringing this ancient wisdom into your modern life will result in spiritual success, abundance, and maybe even a few miracles.

This book is divided into four parts. In part 1, we begin by preparing you for your magical journey. You will be introduced to mystical tools that will be utilized throughout the book, and this section will teach you how to implement them successfully and make the most of them. You will also receive our suggestions on how best to work with the altars and meditations in the following chapters.

In parts 2 and 3, we will be introducing seven extraordinary archetypes, including deities and animal guides, that can help you tap into your unlimited potential. Although there are many guides you can work with from the East, we were guided to choose these seven archetypes; we did an asking ceremony, in which we invited the divine teachers who would like to be a part of our book to show up, and we channeled their messages and teachings into this book. The guides who are part of each chapter share powerful commands that you can activate for healing and manifesting.

The seven archetypes that you will meet and connect with include Tiger, Phoenix, Dragon, Money Frog, Golden Ancestors, Kuan Yin, and Laughing Buddha. If you already work with or understand Asian magic, you would typically think that after Tiger, Phoenix, and Dragon would come Tortoise, because those are the Four Directional Divinities, but that was not the case here—the Money Frog jumped right into our visions and wanted to share its wisdom with you instead. It is important to connect with animal guides in our culture because many North Asian shamanic tribes believe that each culture descended from different animals, and connecting to them is like accessing great origin powers.[1]

These guides will be offering you divine secrets to help you bring in more love, joy, abundance, and beauty, transforming your life like a lotus unfolding its petals. You will be called to sit with your guides for as long as you like, and to ask for the blessings they love to bestow upon us. With their help, you will become more aware of your own inner magic and power.

In part 4, we will introduce a variety of Asian magical modalities and exercises that we have both experienced, which include practices that are Chinese, Taiwanese, and Japanese in origin. We chose well-known modalities in Eastern magical practices, including the introduction of the five elements, the lunisolar zodiac, and crystal feng shui. We've included a few practices from Singapore and America as well.

Part 4 is also focused on expanding further outside of the self, and you will learn how to elevate the energies around you, including your inner circle, your community, and the planet. You will be invited to transform and release limiting beliefs and patterns that may have been difficult to break free from in the past. The gems of wisdom in this book will open doors to new insight and powerful energy streams. Chapter by chapter, you will embark on a unique journey as you reflect, engage, and explore. As part of this mystically guided journey, you will also learn how to create an altar for each specific archetype, meet your personal guides, activate your Sacred Codes with commands and affirmations, and create a ritual for the energies in each chapter.

---

1. Shi, *Spirit Voices*, chap. 2.

Throughout this book, you will be given instructions on how to work with Asian American magic for success, receive answers to important questions, and set up a physical environment that flows with the energy of the Universe to call in your intentions. By the end of this book, you will be able to use ancient magic in a modernized way, to create your own unique revolution, and to live the life of your dreams.

It is important to note that what we share is not the only way to work with this magic. The practices in this book have been a part of Asian culture for centuries. We share the systems and processes we have been called to transmit, as well as others that we have utilized and experienced in our own lives that have supported us on our journeys. *The Mandarin Tree* is not purely traditional Asian folk magic nor is it a representation of all Asian American magic. Instead, this book is like us: a beautiful blend of Asian culture and other practices and beliefs we have adopted along the way.

Most importantly, we really want you to have fun working with the enchanted guides, archetypes, and deities we introduce to you, and we hope that, through the guidance we provide, you will build your magical practice. We also want you to know there is no right or wrong way to work with magic; whatever resonates most for you is divinely perfect for you. Allow yourself the freedom to discover your individual magic—it will transform your life!

Now, let's connect with our inner magic and begin to explore the energies in this book. Anything you desire is already yours—it is time to claim it.

To infinite possibilities!

Samantha + Pamela xo

Part One
Preparing for Your Magical Journey

Chapter One
Your Guide to Magical Success

❁

Everything is difficult in the beginning.
—Chinese Proverb

Whether you are a new mystical practitioner or an experienced one, you will want to check out this chapter and the next prior to beginning your journey. This section will introduce you to, and provide an understanding of, the many magical tools and processes we have integrated into this book to enhance your experience.

All of the meditations, altar work, activation practices, and journal prompts we have integrated in each chapter have been channeled by both of us for the purpose of creating a powerful and transformational experience for you. We have incorporated a beautiful blend of both traditional practices and modern modalities. Our hope is that you will read what we offer, take what resonates most with you, and then add your own flavor of magic to these practices. Magic is ever-changing, and everyone has their own way of connecting to their practices. What we share in *The Mandarin Tree* is to be used as a guide; it is not the only way of working with deities or magical archetypes. The most important thing is to trust your own intuition. Allow yourself to add—or take away—anything that does not keep you in the magical flow.

In each chapter, there are many actions you can take to activate the connection with your guides. If you are an overachiever like we are, you can do all the suggested activities and actions. However, if the options feel a bit overwhelming, then just do one or two of the things we share in each chapter.

We encourage you to only work with the guides and deities that genuinely light you up inside. When you are truly excited to work with a guide or deity, it strengthens your connection. Keep in mind that different beings may resonate with you at different times. Additionally, pay attention to signs that you should work with a specific guide or deity, even if you don't think you are ready. For example, if you keep seeing frogs after reading about the Prosperity Frog but were unsure if you wanted to work with that particular guide, then that is probably confirmation that you should start working with the Prosperity Frog.

Tools to Elevate Your Consciousness

Throughout the book, we will share several different methods for supporting your connection to your magic. Let us walk you through some of the tools we recommend.

Altars

One of the most powerful practices you can incorporate is having an altar. An altar is a sacred space that gathers more and more power each time you use it to pray or perform magic. It is also a central space for you to focus on your intention. And, for the purposes of this book, your altar allows you to connect with your magical guides at an even deeper level. It is a physical place for your guides to reside, so your connection will be stronger and the messages you receive clearer.

Your altar can be as simple or elaborate as you like. Most of our altars are created on a flat surface like a table, a shelf, or a bookcase. Remember, it is supposed to be a space that lights you up and brings you back to your self and your spiritual connections. Decorate it with things that make you feel calm and inspired. You can use crystals, candles, incense, statues, personal items that reflect the energy you are calling in, anything you find in nature, and whatever your intuition guides you to place on your altar. With that being said, in each of the chapters, we have channeled magical tools and symbols you can include on your altar that coincide with each guide. You may want to include some of them, or you may not. Use your intuition to choose the best items for your altar. Trust your gut.

Cleansing Your Altar

Before you set up your altar, you will first want to cleanse the space. We do this so we can clear any stagnant energies that might be blocking us or our magical work. There are a few easy ways to cleanse your altar space.

Physical cleansing can be done by simply wiping your altar down, both the surface and decorative items. If you want to add an extra energy-clearing step, you can also wipe down your tools and your space with Florida water. You can buy a bottle of Florida water online, or you can get it from a local metaphysical shop. Some people use essential oil sprays to clear the area; you can buy them or make your own at home. Smoke from an herbal wand is an additional way to clear the space around your altar. Light a bundle of herbs and waft the smoke with your hands to move any energies that are not supporting you out of the area. Our favorite herbs to use are rosemary and lavender because these two herbs promote positive vibes and repel negative energy. You can dry herbs to make your own wands, or you can buy them from metaphysical shops.

If you are a healer or know an energetic modality like Reiki, you can also charge your altar space with this beautiful healing energy. Simply imagine a light coming from your heart and enveloping the space (or an item you would like to bless). See the light releasing any negative energies.

There are lots of ways to cleanse your altar space. If you are open to trying different methods, each chapter has specific guidance for how to cleanse your altar in the ritual section.

Taking Down an Altar

When you are finished working with a specific guide or deity and are ready to take down your altar, first thank the guide or deity for being in this space with you. To do this, stand in front of your altar with your hands together, in prayer position, and hold them at your heart. Aloud, thank the guide or deity for supporting you on your magical journey.

After giving thanks, you can start taking down your altar. When it comes to magical tools that can be used over and over again such as crystals, candleholders, and other items, you can use smoke from an herbal wand to cleanse them or wipe them down with Florida water. (For items like tarot cards, smoke cleansing would be best.) If you have items that can be discarded, such as food or flowers, they should be disposed of safely. We like to dispose of flowers by placing them outside to give the magic back to the earth, but you could also throw them in your compost bin or trash can.

Once an altar has been taken down, you can immediately create your next altar, if you so desire. When you have an activated altar, it is best practice to clean the space daily, weekly, or whenever your intuition guides you to. Remember, this is a sacred space for you and your guides, so show respect by keeping it tidy and clean.

Tarot

One of the magical tools we utilize on our altars is tarot. Tarot is a system of seventy-eight cards that can be used for personal or spiritual development, intuitive predictions, magical work, and more. On its own, tarot is a powerful portal for the energies you want to invoke, and when it is combined with the magic of altar work, it is amplified even more.

Each tarot deck is composed of major arcana cards, minor arcana cards, and court cards. There are twenty-two major arcana cards. If your life was an Asian drama and you were the main character, then these cards would be the cast of main and supporting characters, or the main plot points of your show. In the minor arcana, there are four suits or houses, which are the Wands, Cups, Swords, and Pentacles. In an Asian drama, these would represent the smaller events that happen in life, like daily routines, driving to work, hanging out with friends, or getting a haircut. The sixteen court cards, four for each suit, illustrate evolution. Court cards ascend from Page to Knight, Queen, and King. These cards represent different stages of your experience or the different personalities of you and the people around you. These would be bigger events in an Asian drama, like finding out you have a long-lost sister, meeting the parents for the first time, or hearing a CEO's son declare his love for you.

In the altar section of each chapter, we have shared specific tarot cards that correlate with that particular guide. You can draw the selected card from your deck and put it on your altar to amplify the energy or help you call in the guide that you are working with. In this book, we are using only major arcana cards on our altars because we are focusing on creating big shifts in our lives by working with these powerful archetypes.

Crystals

Crystals are another magical tool we love to work with. These beautiful rocks are naturally attuned to energy and can help us heal, shift, and expand. When you work with crystals as a tool, what you are manifesting or creating will be amplified. Just as you cleanse and clear your altar space, the same is true of your crystals. Crystals should be cleansed after you are finished using them—don't clear the energy of the crystal while you are working with it, because you want the magic to build up.

You can cleanse crystals with an herbal wand of rosemary or lavender, essential oil spray, or light from the full moon. Moonlight from a full moon is one of the most powerful ways to cleanse crystals and can reset any energies that the crystal has picked up. A few more ways to cleanse crystals are to place them in a bowl of salt, set them next to a selenite crystal (selenite is self-cleansing), or bathe them under the sunlight or the moonlight. Setting a simple intention that the crystal is charged with your own power and energy will also cleanse it. Last, you could wash the crystal with running water or water that was charged under the full moon. Keep in mind that certain crystals don't do well in water, so make sure you research the crystal before choosing this method.

In each chapter, we will provide guidance on how to use crystals as part of your altar, as well as suggestions for which ones to use with certain guides. Know that you don't have to go out of your way to get all of the crystals we list. If you don't have a particular crystal, you can use a clear quartz instead, as it can be a substitute for other crystals' energies.

Sometimes we like to keep a crystal with us after we take down our altar so that the energy of a guide and/or ritual can still be accessed. You might need some joyful energy from the Laughing Buddha or assistance from your Golden Ancestors from time to time. Hold on to that crystal and its energy for as long as you need. Just make sure to cleanse and reset the crystal before you use it for something new.

Meditation

After you have set up your altar, you can choose to activate the connection to your guides via meditation. Each chapter has a specific meditation for that deity and magical archetype. The best way to experience these meditations is to record it yourself reading it aloud and then playing it back. This way, you can simply focus on listening. Plus, you will be easily guided into the meditation by the sound of your own voice. If you'd rather just read the meditation first and then take the journey yourself with an overview of the meditation in mind, that can be magical too.

Sacred Code Activations

Toward the end of each chapter, you will find Sacred Code Activations. This section has commandments for each guide as well as mantras, ascension prompts, and channeled messages. These Sacred Code Activations were channeled by us and are not something you will find in traditional Asian folk magic. Working with Sacred Codes has been a potent tool for us and has led to massive transformation, so we wanted to share this important part of our magic with you. These powerful energy transmissions connect you to your own internal superpowers.

The commandments are a way for you to create a stronger connection to your guides. When we ask is when we shall receive. These commandments are considered a strong asking to connect with your guides. Using the commandments creates a strong vibrational link between you and your guides. It's giving the Universe a clear message that you'd like to receive their love, support, and guidance at this time. It's giving yourself permission to receive, and your guides permission to gift and give.

Mantras are intended to activate your heart energy and transform your mind *and* your heart as you embody your magical work. They allow you to continue your work with your guides after you have completed a ritual. From our list of suggested mantras, choose one you can repeat when you want to get back into alignment with your guides or your magic. Mantras are vibrations spoken through your voice, so you do have to say them out loud. Speak the mantra, sing it, or chant it for however long you'd like; we like to chant until it puts us into a trancelike state and we can feel the vibrations buzzing in our entire body. You may experience downloads of wisdom while reading, writing, or chanting the mantra. These downloads may be a sudden spark of inspiration, a new idea, a new emotion, or even a new way of being.

Once you are finished repeating the mantra, you can grab a journal and tap into your creative flow using the prompts provided. Ascension prompts spark imagination and reveal new ways of thinking, feeling, and seeing the world.

Lastly, chapters have a channeled message from each guide. These are powerful, direct transmissions that seal in all of the magic that you've just built up while working your way through the chapter. These messages can also support you whenever you need some wisdom or encouragement. Rereading them is a great way to start or end your day.

This Is *Your* Journey

Working with Asian American magic is all about finding alignment and flow. While we make suggestions, don't feel you need to lock yourself into a schedule and do magic at a certain time. Magic builds the more you practice it, but it works best when you do it in a way that feels good to you. If keeping a schedule and visiting your altar every morning feels right for you, then do it. If that feels really constricting, maybe even like a chore, then simply visit your altar when you feel inspired and excited to.

The same is true of ritual work. We provide a multitude of ideas, suggestions, and practices to assist you as you learn about and work with the guides and deities integral to this book, but you should never feel obligated to do anything. Sometimes, we include specific guidelines or timings for a ritual, but it is up to you to decide when you want to do them. Ultimately, this is your journey, so we encourage you to do what resonates most with you each step of the way. We believe that following your heart will lead to a profound and life-changing experience.

Part Two
Mystical Beings and Animal Magic

Chapter Two
The Tiger

❀

Even when a girl is as shy as a mouse,
you still have to beware of the tiger within.
—CHINESE PROVERB

Far East Tiger deities appear in many different forms and colors. The Tiger is mentioned in many Chinese, Japanese, and Korean legends, and this version of the Tiger archetype is the specific energy we will be invoking in this chapter. Taiwanese folklore passed down to us shared that the Tiger was so powerful, it was the only guardian allowed to fight alongside the Dragon, who was seen as the Emperor of the Animal Kingdom. (Tiger often appears with Dragon, an archetype we will introduce in chapter 4.) These stories emphasized the strength, power, grace, and royalty of the beloved Tiger. In fact, in the Taiwanese stories and teachings we grew up with, the magical Tiger god is referred to as the "King of the Mountains." The shape of the stripes on the head of the Tiger are how you write the Chinese word for king (王).

Our favorite story of the Tiger is the amazing race in the Chinese zodiac, held by the Jade Emperor. (You will learn more about the Chinese zodiac race in chapter 9.) The story explains why there are only twelve zodiac animals and how this came to be. You see, a long time ago there were no zodiac guides, so the Jade Emperor decided a race would select twelve animals to become his guardians.

The first part of the race involved competing on land. Tiger started off strong: he was powerful, fast, and graceful, and he made it through the forest in no time. Often, this part of the race is not mentioned because the important part of the story takes place during the last obstacle, which was to swim across a river. This was much more of a challenge for many of the animals, especially Tiger. Tiger, like most cats, did not enjoy the water, so it took him awhile to get across. He persevered and ultimately came in third place. Finishing in the top twelve earned him a permanent spot on the Chinese zodiac. As a result, anyone born in the Year of the Tiger is said to be loyal, charming, brave, and competitive—and you will see why, once you begin to engage with Tiger energy.

When working with the energies of the Tiger, you will feel a boost of confidence. You will also feel very motivated to pursue your dreams; as the Tiger will show you, goals can be reached instantaneously with one powerful leap. The Tiger god can also be invoked when you need protection. All you need to do is pray and ask for courage, guidance, or assistance to overcome a challenging situation.

Tiger Magic

Tiger magic is the fire burning inside each one of us. This magic is dormant until the pressures of life fan the flames during intense moments that require power and presence, like a mom lifting a car off of a baby. As you work with Tiger magic, you will feel flickers of this powerful energy.

Tiger magic is also the ferocious creativity that activates when the cosmos intervenes in your life, powerfully protecting you by providing a course correction. With every challenge and perceived difficulty in life, your shadow is being chiseled in order to make room for more of your own divine light.

Without a connection to Tiger magic, you may find yourself feeling lost, hopeless, and without direction, swimming inside other people's imaginations and being pulled left and right according to their agendas. Instead of being secure in your own direct connection to Source Energy—instead of using your precious life force energy to accomplish your own dreams—you may find your energy leaking out via people pleasing. Tiger magic focuses on a powerful message: the purpose of life force energy is to pursue your own dreams and desires so that you can enjoy your accomplishments and successfully work with others to that end; tapping into the energy of the Tiger powerfully redirects you to this path when you have gone astray.

In the societal world, it is easy to get pulled into the ideas and goals of people around us, but Tiger magic reminds us of our sovereign inner authority. Your Tiger magic contains your divine truth, a unique blueprint and life path designed specifically for you. While others may be able to be an example and guide you, your inner authority is the only one that can help you connect with your ultimate truth.

We live in an age where we are our own gurus. You are the one who will lead yourself through the darkness and into the light. There will always be those who are meant to support you and be a part of your journey, but your divine truth is a power that lives deeply within you. Tiger magic will bring you back to this clarity over and over again.

The Tiger is ready to fight for your burning desires, even when you have a hard time fighting for yourself—he is there with you every step of the way. His strength will bring you comfort and power at the same time. Allow his courage, boldness, and bravery to inspire you. The innate gift of your own power was given to you by the Universe when you were born, and it will forever be with you. Treasure this special gem and its connection to Tiger magic.

Samantha's Tiger Story

As a visionary, there are few things more exciting than a new project or seeing your imagination come to life. Perhaps most exciting is getting to create something with your best friends. In my mid-thirties I decided I really wanted to be in business with a group of women, women who could create an out-of-this-world coaching business together and genuinely support each other over a lifetime. I remember pitching the idea to my potential business partners with this zest for life: "How exciting will it be to support each other over an entire lifetime?!" After weeks of deep and intentional conversations, four of us sisters decided to come together to create a very magical business.

After a couple of years of business branding, website building, program creations, photoshoots, meetings, creation sessions, tears and tough conversations, and receiving so much coaching ourselves, we had to face the hard truth that the business just wasn't working. For whatever reason, it didn't matter how we tried to promote our programs—they just never fully took off.

While the finance side of things wasn't panning out so well, the experience was truly beautiful. The four of us had so many magical dinners and goddess gatherings, including a life-changing trip to London where we learned from extraordinary teachers and had countless moments filled with laughter. We grew so much together and stepped into even more powerful versions of ourselves, and yet the gloomy truth was that the business's income didn't allow us to continue working together. We poured so much heart, love, and energy into it that it was hard to walk away. When you know in your heart and soul that something isn't quite right for you, but you love it anyway, those are the most difficult situations to gather the courage to walk away from.

One day, Tiger magic came to me in meditation. It was time. It was time to do something really brave and courageous, even if the process wasn't going to be enjoyable. I knew it would be a moment of liberation for all of us. With the Tiger backing me, I brought up the conversation that it might be time for us to part ways. At that point, personal private coaching businesses would make more sense. As I uttered the words, everyone made a sigh of relief. We'd all known it deep down, but we'd wanted to keep moving forward since we loved each other so much. We realized that we had done an incredible job of growing together over the last year. But, like a plant that has grown too big for its pot, it was time for us to move forward and make a change. We all wanted to stay within the cozy comfort of being together, yet we knew that the Universe had other plans for us. Our paths were unique, and it was time for the Tiger to remind each of us of our individual power.

That separation hit me so hard that I had intense lower back pain for an entire month. I didn't really know what was happening, but I knew my body was helping me process the change. Our energies needed space and time to detangle, and the Tiger was with me every step of the way. I kept hearing the Tiger whisper, "You can do this on your own. Keep going." At the time, moments of doubt and hesitation kept popping up: could I really have a business on my own? I had been so reliant on the care, love, and support of my sisters.

The Tiger ignited a fire inside me and reminded me that my purpose, my vision, and my calling were bigger than this temporary rearrangement of energy. The situation may have looked like "failure" in the moment, but really it was just the stepping stone to the next adventure. None of us had failed; in the process, we each found deeper versions of ourselves. It was time to grow in new ways.

As I took the reins and opened a business entirely on my own, an entirely new world started to emerge in front of me. I began to attract a new caliber of clients, and money seemed to just blossom in front of me. I was shocked and amazed, and I didn't know how to receive the amount of goodness flooding in. Again, Tiger reminded me, "Keep going. This is your destiny."

Every time I thought that I needed to take a step back, the Tiger got me moving forward again. "Keep going. Don't stop."

Over and over again, I heard the Tiger's magical voice backing me and keeping me on track. It's like the Universe removed every possible way for me to people please or mold myself into some-one that I wasn't.

I started to believe in my power, and more opportunities presented themselves. Only a few months after the embers of my old business died out and my new business was birthed, I signed my very first book contract with Pamela. It's so wild how the Universe guides you in new ways while making sure you remain on your path. For my internal strength and power, I will always be grateful for Tiger magic.

Tiger magic is a fire and strength that's deep within you, and the flames burn brighter as you get closer and closer to your purpose and destiny. It may not feel comfortable in the moment—that is often the nature of change. Do not be afraid of temporary discomfort. Instead, be grateful that this energy is always available to you. Activating the courage within is what allows this magnificent energy to guide you to the next stop on your journey. When you make space for this natural power to arise from within, you begin to support yourself from the inside out.

Pamela's Tiger Story

There are many stories of the Tiger showing up to help me return to my courageous, powerful self. While they are all impactful, the one I have chosen to share resonates most with the essence of the book. It is also the story the Tiger nudged me to share with you.

The Tiger is about inner strength, being courageous, and going after what you truly desire because you know the object of that desire is meant for you. This can take you out of your comfort zone, which is when you probably feel the most fear or doubt in your life; most of us don't like to be uncomfortable. But pushing beyond your comfort zone can have miraculous results.

One of the biggest leaps in my career as an author, deck creator, and entrepreneur was when I made the life-changing decision to self-publish my first deck, *Crystal Unicorn Tarot*, in 2018. I had actually tried to create multiple decks before that, but they had totally fallen flat, which was very discouraging. During a beautiful meditation and healing, I encountered the amazing world of the Crystal Unicorns, and I just knew that I had to create a deck about it. And, adding to my inspiration, there were no unicorn tarot decks out there—the market was ripe for it. Plus, I desperately wanted a unicorn deck for my own readings.

At the beginning of my Crystal Unicorn journey, all my failed decks resurfaced, making it really hard for me to start the project because I was scared of being unsuccessful again. This is where Tiger magic came in. The Tiger gently pushed me toward my mission and my purpose, letting me know that the past did not define my future or who I was, and that the time was right for me to follow my passions. I became focused on what it was I truly desired, and I knew that my "why" was much more important than all the negative thoughts of the past.

Of course, the Tiger was right. My crowdfunding was a success, and through that process, people started to look for me online and learned about other things I was doing as well, including my coaching business. When *Crystal Unicorn Tarot* was finally published, everyone loved it. It was a huge success, even internationally, with companies from Japan and China contacting me to purchase the deck. As I continued to follow my creative flow, which the Tiger still guided me to, I began to sign contracts for additional decks and books. Now, less than five years later, I have nine publishing contracts! I still love sharing my wisdom and magic through my decks and books. If I had just given up because things got too hard, and had allowed myself to be deterred from my mission, then you would not be reading this book right now.

It's important to know that while the magic of the Tiger is fierce, it is also very protective and nurturing, meaning you will not be pushed into something you don't want to do. The Tiger is always leading you to that which is for your highest good. The courageous actions you are called to take are laid out for you, paw by paw. When you allow yourself to be guided by the majestic wisdom of the Tiger, you are being led to your soul's highest purpose.

Setting Up Your Tiger Altar

Tiger energy is all about loyalty and trust, including knowing when to trust ourselves and when to trust others. Staying loyal to your daily devotions when working with Tiger energy will propel you to your goals. The Tiger is always pleased by the dedication and energy we put toward honoring the fierce Tiger magic within; when we are committed to this work, the Tiger rewards us with amazing results.

Here are some tools related to Tiger energy that you can use to decorate your altar. These suggestions were guided by the Tiger in a meditative channeling that we performed for this book. Feel free to add tools that are familiar to you or any others we have discussed. Always remember the energy of the Tiger is regal, majestic, and related to divine prosperity.

Tiger Crystals

Emerald
Tiger's eye
Sapphire
Jade

Tiger Colors

White
Black
Gold
Blue

Tiger Symbols

Claws
Crowns
Jewelry
Forests

Tiger Food Offerings

Poultry dishes
Eggs
Mangos or fruits with seeds
Sesame seeds

Tiger Tarot Cards

Strength
The Emperor
The Empress

Create a ceremony to honor the Tiger daily. It can be as simple as greeting your Tiger altar every morning while working with Tiger energy, lighting a candle, and speaking an intention for the day. You can stand in front of your altar and recite the commands, affirmations, and mantras at the end of this chapter. If you want to get fancy, you can also be the embodiment of the Tiger: prance or dance around the room as if you are the magnificent Tiger, pouncing on your goals.

After you have finished setting up your beautiful Tiger altar, activate the altar by calling in your Tiger guide using the instructions in the next section.

Meeting Your Tiger Guide

Take a few deep breaths. Settle your body and your mind. Find yourself in your own magical space. It is time to meet your Tiger guardian. Feel a level of cheerfulness as you sink into meditation. You may even imagine that you're sitting under a mandarin tree full of leaves and bright orange fruits.

The powerful paws of the Tiger enter the area, one step at a time. You can feel the immense royal power that flows through Tiger. At a comfortable pace, Tiger approaches you. You feel a warmth and a closeness. Tears may stream down your face as you are reconnected to your inner Tiger power. A surge of energy runs through your body; there may be sparks of electricity or color. In this moment, all limiting beliefs of disempowerment surface, only to be flushed out of the body.

Tiger embraces you in a deep hug, one that shows honor toward you and celebrates your bravery in this lifetime. You get on the back of Tiger, and he roars loudly, making the area around you shudder. Swiftly, Tiger launches you through the inter-dimensional portals of time and space. Opaque rainbow colors stream past as you move at the speed of light. You grab on to Tiger's fur, and he turns around and smiles. Tiger's greatest joy is to be with you.

Tiger takes you to the Temple of the Oracle, the All-Seeing Eye. The temple is gold with incredibly high ceilings. You smell the scent of incense everywhere. Jewels that sparkle and shimmer are all around you. Tiger majestically walks through the doors of the Temple of the Oracle. The Mage of Light greets you and walks you closer to the Empress. The Empress is a gorgeous White Tiger, glistening with light. She walks toward you and places her paw over your third eye. A wave of electricity flows through you. You begin to see your lifetimes flash before your eyes.

When the Empress removes her paw from your forehead, there is a jewel in her paw. "This is the Jewel of the Great Oracle," she says. "It will reclaim all of your strength and your power from the seven dimensions of lifetimes. It will completely clear karmic patterns, distractions, and illusions that have been holding you back from seeing your own light and strength."

Layers of heavy thoughts and feelings shake loose and leave your body. The Empress then says, "This is complete." She smiles warmly at you.

You feel a fullness and a level of confidence that was not available to you before. You are becoming aware of how many challenges you overcame throughout several past lives. Your strength and power flood back to you. A new wisdom has awakened within you, through the power of the Jewel of the Great Oracle. An integration occurs. You are initiated.

Tiger appears at your side and greets you. It's time to rest now. Sleepily, you get on Tiger's back again, and he flies you through the inter-dimensional portal. You need time to absorb all that you have learned. Tiger brings you back to your room and tucks you into bed. Then, he gives you a message: "I am always with you. Tiger magic and Tiger power are always with you. Call upon me, and I will be here for you."

As the world of Tiger fades into soft opalescent lights in the background of your mind, you find yourself coming back to yourself and the room you are in. Gently move your fingers and toes as you reintegrate with the powerful present moment. Things have shifted and changed. You're no longer the same person. Layers of power, courage, and bravery have energetically been restored to your consciousness. You may notice yourself sitting a little taller and walking a little straighter. There's a new level of universal support that's now available for you, and you may experience this in the way you speak, in your cadence or your tone of voice. The words you choose to speak will have more courage infused in them. The power of the Roaring Tiger is inside of you now. The frequency of this new strength will walk with you in this lifetime.

Roaring Tiger Ritual

The Tiger wants to share a very powerful ritual to take back your power and break free of needing others' approval to succeed. This ritual is to be done only on the first Sunday of the month. The reason for this is because in Chinese, Sunday is written as the word *sky*, and the Tiger wants to let you know that anything is possible—the sky's the limit! Actually, there are no limits, because you are a cosmic energetic being that can co-create anything you desire. We are the most powerful manifesters when we are confident and sure of ourselves, so this ritual will empower you and strengthen your belief in yourself and your ability to succeed at anything you put your mind to. Get ready to claim your Tiger magic, and let them hear you roar.

To prep for the ritual, you will first need to connect with your Tiger guide using the meditation in the previous section of this chapter. Afterward, gather these magical tools:

Tiger figurine or picture

Your intention (what you will accomplish after you have stepped into your sacred power)

Small piece of paper

Pen

Salt of your choice

Plate

Three white candles

Lighter or matches

Crystal (optional)

Cleanse your sacred space and Tiger altar with an herbal wand or spray and set up your magical tools for the ritual. Make sure you are in a place where you won't be disturbed for the duration of your ritual. Your ritual can be as long as you want, depending on the time you want to stay in the energy of the Tiger and the size of your candles.

1. Write your intention on the small piece of paper and fold it once toward you, calling back all your power and magic.

2. Sitting in front of your magical tools and altar, put your written intention under the Tiger figurine or picture. If you have a crystal you would like to add to this ritual, feel free to set the crystal next to the figurine/on top of the picture.

3. Set your plate in front of your intention. Using as much salt as you need, draw the Chinese character representing the king (王) on the plate. Here are instructions for writing the character:

   • Make a horizontal line.
   • Make another horizontal line directly below.

- Starting at the middle of the top line, draw a vertical line going down through the line beneath and extending beyond it.
- Draw a horizontal line at the bottom of the vertical line.

4. Put your three candles at each of the points where the horizontal line meets the vertical line. The three candles should be down the center of your plate.

5. Before you light your candles, place your hands over the plate and say your intention out loud three times. Say it loud and proud, letting the Universe hear you roar.

6. When you are ready, light your three candles, starting at the top of the plate. As you are lighting each candle, say your intention in your mind with confidence.

7. When you are done lighting your candles, visualize your success being played out in your mind. See yourself achieving all your goals, standing in your power, and letting Tiger magic guide you to victory.

8. Allow the candles to burn themselves out. Never leave candles unattended. If you need to leave the space, make sure you snuff them out first; when you relight each candle, say your intention again.

9. When the candles have burned out, that is when your ritual is finished. Gather the salt, intention paper, and any leftover wax. You can keep everything on your altar or throw it away. Keep your Tiger figurine (or photo) on your altar, or carry it with you, for good luck.

Do this ritual whenever you need a boost of personal power, always on the first Sunday of the month.

Sacred Code Activations

The Tiger Guardian is always available to you and is activated from within yourself. When you'd like to activate more power, more courage, and more boldness in your Universe, we invite you to call upon the Tiger Commandment. This is a powerful statement to yourself and the Universe that you're inviting in the magic of Tiger and are ready to receive his direct energy and support.

Tiger Commandment

"Powerful Tiger guardian, as a direct expression of the Divine, I ask for your fiery ferociousness to purify my consciousness and bring me back to truth. I ask that all illusions and delusions be cleared from my mind, my body, and my emotions. Bring me back to the truth of my soul's essence and my powerful soul expression. Remind me of my power, my strength, and my light. Guide me back onto my path with gusto and speed. Dissolve and dismantle all distractions, people-pleasing tendencies, energy leaks, and doubtful thoughts from my mind. Bring me back to this powerful moment, and keep me focused on my personal path of truth. I am available for all guidance and messages. Teach me to be available to hear, feel, and listen. I allow the power of the Tiger guardian to be with me now. Bring me back to the highest expression of good. And so it is."

Tiger Mantras

Use a Tiger mantra to keep your energy focused on a specific feeling that activates and awakens your inner strength and power. Stay with the mantra long enough to calibrate yourself to this new energetic field. The correct mantra for you will elicit a feeling of power inside. The moment that the mantra feels neutral, or no longer has a feeling connected to it for you, then you have graduated from this mantra and are ready for the next. You can come up with your own Tiger mantra, or choose one from the following list:

- I am allowed to be strong and in my power.
- I get to powerfully decide what my truth is.
- I have permission to fully listen to my powerful intuition.
- I trust my intuition to guide me.
- Being in my strength is a good thing.
- I am now standing in my power.
- My power is for the good of all.
- I create only win-win situations.
- My power is a stream of energy flowing through me from the Universe.
- Power is my natural birthright.

You may find yourself coming back to these mantras in a month (or even a year), only to find that the mantras have a new layer of meaning for you at that time. Let yourself play with these energies for a lifetime. Calibrate back to them whenever you need. Mantras will continue to elevate and empower you.

Tiger Ascension Prompts

Tiger energy is a power that you awaken and activate within yourself. Use these ascension prompts to awaken those new levels of powers within. You can write responses in a journal or spend time in self-reflection. You may want to light a candle and have your favorite tea or beverage close by. Spend some time with yourself, diving deep into self-exploration. See yourself becoming more and more powerful as you unravel the following questions:

1. If you allowed yourself to fully express yourself, what would that look and feel like? Tap into the version of yourself that grants you permission to share, speak, teach, and express yourself to the public. Write exactly what you want to say, and exactly how you want to come across to others. What did that feel like? What would change if you allowed your fullest expression to come through?

2. If you were to powerfully take a stand for something in your life, what would that be? Is there something that you absolutely know is for you? Are you ready to claim it now? Why or why not?

3. Where are you giving your power away and discrediting yourself? Get crystal clear. What is one action you can take each day that is fully aligned to who you are in order to bring you back to integrity?

4. When things get you down, how do you lift yourself back up? What is your strategy to bring yourself back to the light? How can you coach yourself to choose powerful

thoughts and words? What would happen if you told your-self more empowering stories about everything that is happening in your life?

Channeled Message from the Tiger

"Your commanding roar is to be heard throughout the earth. You are here to claim your throne and claim your space. The energy of your voice creates worlds, and it deserves to be heard. Be in your power, and the Universe will bend to your will."

—TIGER

Chapter Three
The Phoenix

❋

A fall in the ditch makes you wiser.
—CHINESE PROVERB

A spark of fire ignites from the ashes and forms a beautiful fowl, the Phoenix, filled with magic and power. The Phoenix can blast through any barrier and ascend to any realm. The energy of this mythical guide is pure and illuminating. Learning from the Phoenix will test you in many ways, so be ready to step out of your comfort zone and do things you previously thought you could never do. Every action you take, every decision you make, will be an exciting adventure—if you allow yourself to soar to your highest potential.

As you work with the Phoenix, be aware of exciting opportunities and shifts happening in your physical world, and happening fast! These will be the indicators that your energetic vibrations are ascending to another level and will signal your rebirth. Some of these changes will be subtle, like cleaning out your closet, or perhaps changing the way you part your hair; other shifts will seem to happen for no apparent reason. Keep in mind that you do not need to rush the rebirth process. Allow yourself to rise gracefully from the ashes, with gratitude for every moment.

The primary wisdom the Phoenix will share with you has to do with activating and trusting your inner compass so that you will be able to more intuitively feel what's right for you, looking within instead of seeking external validation. When you focus on rising from the ashes, you will stop trying to please society, or even your loved ones, because you will be guided by your true desires. Pay attention to every spark of passion that comes from deep within your soul as well as direct messages from the cosmos. Your purpose in life is not to please those around you, but rather to listen to the powerful, invisible guidance from within.

The legend of the Phoenix can be found in many cultures, especially in Chinese mythology. We were brought up to believe that there are several versions of the Phoenix. In this chapter, we will connect with the energy of the Phoenix found in Chinese mythology, also known as *Fenghuang*, which is infused into many stories and traditions in China and Taiwan. Some of these stories originated long ago, when there were dynasties and ruling emperors. These majestic birds can also be found in ancient pottery, architecture, and artwork, where the Phoenix symbol is often, significantly, associated with royalty. In modern times, the Phoenix still has an influence in many Chinese dramas, movies, and television series.

In one of the ancient Chinese Scriptures, *Erya*, the Phoenix is depicted as having "the beak of a rooster, the face of a swallow, the forehead of a fowl, the neck of a snake, the breast of a goose, the back of a tortoise, the hindquarters of a stag, and the tail of a fish."[2] It is known to be an auspicious totem in Chinese culture, which means it is a sign of good luck. The Phoenix also represents the six celestial bodies: the head symbolizes the sky, the eyes are the burning sun, the back of the Phoenix is the moon, the wings are swift like the wind, the tails are the planets, and the feet are the grounding earth. In modern times, you will see the Phoenix represented at important Chinese events, such as weddings.

Phoenix Magic

Phoenix magic is a light that shines deep within our soul and awakens our actualized self. It is the cosmic fire of creation available to every single one of us, though sometimes it is buried very deep within. This energy guides our soul's desires and whispers wisdom to us in our quiet, everyday moments; it is a direct connection to Source energy, gifted to us at the moment of our birth. The immune system is evidence of this light warrior within us: it knows exactly when the tiniest foreign particle is not in alignment with our individual system, and it begins the clearing-away process. In contrast, when the immune system recognizes something akin to our individual makeup, it will protect it and keep it safe.

---

2. Cultural-china.com, "Chinese Phoenix—Auspicious Bird Rising from Ashes."

This Phoenix fire magic is potent in small children. Children who gravitate toward singing, dancing, writing, playing a musical instrument, or obsessing over sports have a stream of energy inside that is guiding them to their natural gifts and talents. When we nurture, nourish, and cultivate this energy, we allow it to evolve to its fullest potential. Often, children don't have the mentors or the guidance to truly allow this magic to awaken within themselves, and many people find that years into their adulthood, they are finally allowing themselves to be who they were born to be. Examples of this are the husband who has a midlife crisis and decides to quit his job and travel the world, or the wife who decides to go back to school to study what she's actually passionate about. These were gifts that went unexpressed, and at some point, the Phoenix's fire will demand life to set itself free. The potential of the soul is a fire that cannot be extinguished.

This unique energy radiates from each of us when we express our soul's truth. Speaking, singing, dancing, and acting in accordance with your profound inner truth radiates from your auric field. This energy emanates an energetic and inaudible sound that can also have an impact on the people around you. When you allow yourself to be your most whole and freely expressed self, you bring balance and harmony to the planet.

The loss of our innate wisdom often happens through societal and parental conditioning. It is easy to squash the light that was gifted to us by the cosmos when we are trying to stay safe and please the people around us. We may forget to tend the fires within. The navigational system meant to direct our every move may go offline due to the external pressure of whatever version of success has been driving us. True success can only be defined from within. It's a state of being in which our deep inner knowing and connection to wholeness allows the correct people, things, and situations to be attracted into our lives.

The power of Phoenix magic is that she has a way of raising you up from the ashes. In your deepest, darkest moments is when your real power arrives. You may feel completely lost, hopeless, and weighed down by the multiple belief systems and personalities that you had to take on to survive. As you burn away the false images, you will reconnect with your powerful self. In the ashes, all that is left is your core and your truth. True wealth, true energy, and true power come from this very deep connection to your core soul essence.

As you allow your inner Phoenix to rise, you will see beyond the dense illusion of reality. Reality is the world you exist in that has already been created; it was constructed by the wants and needs of your loved ones and other influences. Reality is also shaped by movies and other media, which have shown us the way things are "supposed to" be. But these are actually repeated and recycled images from the past. To be in congruence with the Phoenix, you must be bold and brave in such a way that you are living on the cutting edge. You must see yourself in a world that is becoming, but perhaps not yet created. When you walk the path of the Phoenix, you see beyond the reality that has been constructed—you see the mystical and magical world of the yet-to-be. It takes boldness and braveness to live here, but once you are connected to this energy, there is no other way to be.

The Phoenix realm is where the artists, innovators, writers, and leaders of our time live. Each possess a deep knowing that they are meant to create something powerful and magical. These creations will not necessarily impress or change the world in an extraordinary way, but they are priceless nonetheless. Creation is a feeling, a spark of life, through which we get to feel the significance of our existence. This spark is always available to us and, when tended, can ignite a fire.

Samantha's Phoenix Story

Growing up in a mixed culture created mixed signals. When I lived in the United States, I was taught that it would be better for me to be loud and funny, to take up space and attract attention. In Taiwan, I was praised for being quiet, carefully pouring tea, being a good listener, and simply being in the background as an observer.

To fit in, I took on both personas. I did my best with both and shifted gears when I traveled from country to country. It took a lot of energy. I second-guessed myself a lot, because I wasn't sure what actions and decisions would be most admired or accepted. Instead of tuning in to my inner Phoenix, I often observed subtle facial expressions and read the room to decide how to show up in any given situation or circumstance. *What do I need to say or do to be more loved and accepted? What do I need to do to make sure I don't get in trouble, get yelled at, or receive a disapproving response? How do I need to show up to get more attention, or the "right" kind of attention? What do I need to do to keep myself safe?* These were some of the questions I was continually asking myself; they played over and over again in my mind. Without fully realizing it, my brain was assessing all of these things before I acted, and as a result, I ended up being very shy.

I remember something as simple as a question like "Do you want Lucky Charms or Frosted Flakes?" would paralyze me. My response was typically "I don't know, what do you want?" I wanted to make sure that I picked the same thing as others so that I would be liked. I couldn't make my own decisions, and I truly didn't know what I wanted. I had squashed my inner Phoenix so much, I didn't hear her call at all.

What should have been an upsetting memory is that one of my classmates would copy my homework every morning. I remember wanting to please him, while at the same time feeling scared that if I didn't let him copy my homework, he'd stop talking to me. I was also afraid I'd get in trouble at some point if I kept it up, yet I allowed this to continue for a whole year. My fear of loss was greater than my need for my truth. All my mixed emotions stayed within me and began to build up. As emotional signals get mixed up and inner power begins to weaken, it is at this point that the body begins to break down. In my case, this resulted in intense skin problems.

There is a concept in Traditional Chinese Medicine that anger overheats the body internally and creates excess phlegm. In my younger years, I ended up having a great deal of acne on my face, chest, and back, I believe because I had so much built-up anger inside of me that my body was overheating. At the time, however, I would always say that I never got angry. I never felt it. It had been so deeply suppressed that it turned into red skin and inflamed acne that was so bad, no acne cream could ever wash it away.

As I became aware of this in my early twenties, I began to fight for myself. I remember the moment I allowed myself to feel anger for the very first time. It was so overwhelming that I just sobbed and screamed and let it all out in front of the mirror. At that moment, I noticed something: while all my emotions were being released, my eyes became sparkly. I started really seeing my true self. I raged and began the process of letting it all out; every suppressed tear streamed down my face. My skin healed, and the redness began to disappear.

I had let too many people take and use my energy for their own benefit, and I wasn't respecting myself or my boundaries. I was giving all of me away. I had no idea what it meant to follow my desires or to truly do the things that lit me up and made me happy. I was so concerned with everyone else's well-being and happiness that I put myself last. I didn't realize that by not taking care of myself, I also couldn't fully show up for the people that I loved.

Being your actualized self is the power of the Phoenix. You have to make powerful choices and decisions yourself, and then allow the Phoenix to clear away and destroy what no longer serves you. The Phoenix fights for your destiny, because you have one. Every person does. This is important: no one can guide you better than your own inner magic can.

Pamela's Phoenix Story

I always say that before a breakthrough, there is often a breakdown. At times, we have to burn through what is not needed in our life—and maybe even watch it go up in flames—for us to get to the rebirthing phase, just like the Phoenix rising from the ashes. The next version of ourselves will be more expansive than the one we left behind. For this reason, we cannot fear the moments when things fall apart.

Since the beginning of 2022, there have been lots of moments like this in my life, including having to start my business over again from ground zero at a time when I was feeling the unhealthiest I'd ever felt. Many things came out of the shadows and demanded my attention. My understanding of my purpose and mission was changing. Important decisions that did not feel good in the moment were pushing me to make a course correction. Even though I was scared of the unknown and a new life, the Phoenix assured me that in order to become reborn, I had to release what was not needed.

What I believe to be true is that there is unlimited potential waiting for each of us. Circumstances in life can change suddenly, and breakthroughs are always right around the corner. Of course, we have to show up in real life and do the work; we can't just eat chips all day and scroll on social media. But what I have learned through many rebirths, breakdowns, and breakthroughs is that it all happens a lot easier if we lead with energy and magic. You see, that magical spark of what you most desire is a GPS to good health and good fortune. If you can allow your Phoenix magic to awaken and lead, you can tap into the flow of the Universe. When you are going with the flow, opportunities, people, and experiences show up easily because you are choosing to encounter them. They have always been there, but you had to remove some obstacles first to realize it.

In 2022, when I allowed myself to open my wings, fly like the Phoenix, and follow my burning desires, magic happened. I released everything I had initially built in my business at the beginning of that year, even though it was my only source of income and I was really scared. I also lost over fifteen pounds I had gained, which had been weighing on me. Everything worked out in my favor, even though I was a bit worried initially. Miracles and blessings that I didn't even know existed were put in front of me, things I never thought possible. I rose from the ashes and continue to rise, and the sky's the limit!

Once I removed the old stories and self-sabotaging thoughts that were blocking the way forward, I was able to fully step into who I authentically am in my relationships and in my business.

I get to play with magic, teach about magical guides like the Phoenix, show up with my rainbow-colored hair, and even wear galactic space suits for photo shoots. I have traveled to amazing places and had a fabulous time in each. By following my intuition and leading from my desires, what could have ended up being a difficult year actually ended with great success as my authentic self was allowed to shine through!

If you also have tough breakdowns prior to breakthroughs, know that it doesn't have to be that way. We do not always have to suffer to achieve our dreams. When I remembered to call upon the power of the Phoenix to quickly burn away what was no longer needed and to help me rise gracefully and easily from the ashes, I discovered this. I also learned that it is okay to welcome the tension and resistance before your rebirth, because the magic and abundance waiting for you on the other side will be so amazing, it is worth it!

Setting Up Your Phoenix Altar

Your Phoenix altar is here to support you and remind you to always follow your inner voice and desire, lead with joy, and be the majestic Phoenix that you are. Whenever you feel confused, frustrated, or stuck, visit this Phoenix altar to get back on track.

Here are some tools related to Phoenix energy that you can use to decorate your altar. These suggestions were guided by the Phoenix in a meditative channeling that we performed for this book. Feel free to add tools that are familiar to you or any others we have discussed. Always remember the energy of the Phoenix is bold, graceful, courageous, and resilient.

Phoenix Crystals

Carnelian
Citrine
Red agate
Orange calcite
Ruby

Phoenix Colors

Red
Yellow
Orange
Gold

Phoenix Symbols

Feathers
Fire
Salt lamps
Jeshanna lily

Phoenix Food Offerings

Citrus fruits or drinks
Green leafy vegetables
Red or orange candy
Spicy flavoring

Phoenix Tarot Cards

Death
Temperance
Wheel of Fortune

Create a ceremony to honor the Phoenix daily. It can be as simple as greeting your Phoenix altar every morning while working with Phoenix energy, lighting a candle, and speaking an intention for the day. You can stand in front of your altar and recite the commands, affirmations, and mantras at the end of this chapter. If you want to get fancy, you can also be the embodiment of the Phoenix: fly or dance around the room as if you are a powerful, beautiful Phoenix spreading your wings.

After you have finished setting up your gorgeous Phoenix altar, activate the altar by calling in your Phoenix guide using the instructions in the next section.

Meeting Your Phoenix Guide

This beautiful meditation will help you spread your intuitive wings and connect to your Phoenix guide to activate your inner fire and actualized self. After your initial introduction to the Phoenix, you may call upon this guide for help any time of the day.

Take a moment to create a sacred space or come to your altar. Play your favorite music, light your favorite candle, and if you want, have your journal close by in case messages are transmitted directly to you. Create space that allows for a miracle to occur. Remember that at any moment you can always invite in the energy and magic of the mandarin tree for extra nourishment and support.

Take a few deep breaths. Settle your body and your mind. Then, see a vibrant, reddish orange, fiery light entering the room. You feel a warm sensation pulsing through your body. With every inhale and exhale, you begin to feel the fires of purification throughout your body. The limitations, the lack, the programming that's no longer serving your system, are all being brilliantly burned away by this fiery light.

As this light washes over you, the veil becomes thinner and you see your Phoenix guide. As she swoops in through the window and enters your space, you see her spreading her courageous wings. Large and bold, you feel her presence. An immense warmth and love emanate from her.

Phoenix whisks you away on a journey into your own powerful unknown. She takes you on a journey back in time, and in those quiet moments, you allow essential memories with messages to appear. Phoenix then shows you aspects of yourself that have always been powerful in the past and offers you an alternative of what is possible for you. You see the same memories float by again, but this time you see the power and courage radiating from you.

Moment by moment, you see red, orange, yellow, and gold lights infusing your past timeline, bringing energy to the parts of you that are ready to see your past from a new perspective. As the energies shift and adjust, observe yourself upgrading moment by moment. Times when you saw yourself as frail transform with this new awareness, and you begin to realize how strong and powerful you were even in those moments. The murkiness clears from your eyes, and you begin to see the truth again—the truth of your power, your energy, and your light. In her bold strength, Phoenix has helped you clearly see who you really are.

Phoenix stares you directly in the face with the warmest expression of love. Then, she takes you to see your future and the version of yourself that awaits. This version of you takes inspired actions, says the brave things, does the bold things, and listens to the whispers of intuition that show up. The new version of you awakens and rises like the fiery Phoenix. It's you in your fullest and boldest expression. As your most authentic self emerges, you embrace the fire and power of the moment while softly surrendering to the moment at the same time.

Phoenix gently gazes at you and tears of joy sparkle from her eyes. She knows that you now see yourself the way she sees you. Phoenix whispers that you can receive insights from her at any time—she is the fire that lives inside you. You are not separate; she is a part of you, and you a part of her. The red, orange, yellow, and gold lights merge within you. Remember the feelings and the energy of this sacred connection, and tap into it to speak with your Phoenix guide at any time.

You find yourself slowly awakening from your dreamy, meditative state. Wiggle your fingertips and toes and find your body warming up with new presence and energy from the Phoenix fire. An orange light and sensation of boldness courses through your entire body. Like the Phoenix rises from the ashes, you are new. Each time you come back to this meditation, you get to be rebirthed as the most current powerful version of yourself.

As you find yourself in this new state of clarity, write down your experience and any messages from your Phoenix. You could also soar to the end of this chapter and respond to the Phoenix Ascension Prompts for deeper insight.

Rising Phoenix Ritual

Before we swoop into this magical ritual, we want to remind you that you are always rebirthing and ascending every single second, of every single minute, of every single day. This ritual is to help you acknowledge and honor all those little moments that add up to a more significant, memorable moment, when your conscious mind becomes aware of your ascension.

As we evolve, our intentions and thoughts dictate where our life is headed. With this ritual, we want you to be able to connect to your intuition and potent inner desires to create your life story even more consciously. It's not about what other people think or want anymore—you are going to manifest your physical reality the way *you* want it and live the life that *you* desire. Trust that if you are reading this, you are ready, and you are in the right place. Let's rise, majestic Phoenix!

To prep for the ritual, you will first need to connect with your Phoenix guide using the meditation in the previous section of this chapter. Afterward, gather these magical tools:

Phoenix drawing or printed picture

Your intention (what connecting to your core self will help you achieve in your life)

Small piece of paper

Red, orange, and yellow pens

Orange candle

Carnelian crystal

Lighter or matches

Cleanse your sacred space and Phoenix altar with an herbal wand or spray and set up your magical tools for the ritual. Make sure you are in a place where you won't be disturbed for the duration of your ritual. Your ritual can be as long as you want, depending on the time you want to stay in the energy of the Phoenix and the size of your candle.

1. Sit in front of your magical tools and your altar. Hold your picture of the Phoenix to your solar plexus, right on your tummy. Call upon your Phoenix guide to appear to you and ask her/him/them to help you activate your inner compass and knowledge. You might imagine or feel your Phoenix arrive, or maybe the room will get hotter. Take as much time as you'd like to converse with and feel connected to the energy of your guide.

2. When you feel you have connected to your Phoenix, set the picture in front of the orange candle.

3. Write out your intention using orange, red, and yellow pens. What do you want to achieve after connecting to your actualized self? Trust your inner voice and make your goals lavish and lush, like the Phoenix!

4. When you are done writing your intention, fold your paper toward you one time, then put it on top of the Phoenix photo. Set your carnelian on top of the intention paper.

5. Now it is time to light the orange candle. Imagine your Phoenix energy rising within you and say your intention out loud as you light your candle.

6. Your ritual will be complete when the candle is finished burning. Make sure you do not leave an open flame unattended. During this time, your energy and connection with the Phoenix will be amplified, so use this opportunity to journal. Allow messages from your core self and your intuition to inspire guidance or instructions that can help you manifest your intention.

7. When the candle has burned out, set the Phoenix picture and intention on your altar so you can visit them every day and remember your purpose. The carnelian is now your Phoenix talisman—whenever you see it or touch it, your connection to your inner compass will deepen even more, allowing you to consciously make decisions from within instead of listening to what other people are telling you to do.

You can recharge your carnelian crystal and do this ritual with a new intention every month. Keep building a beautiful life filled with what you truly want!

Sacred Code Activations

Phoenix fuels the fire that already resides within you, the kind of fire that's required to dissolve and release masks, beliefs, personalities, and identities that have buried you inside of someone else's ideas of who you are and who you were meant to be. The Phoenix Commandment activates a kind of superpower that reminds you of the best version of yourself and reawakens the magic that is sometimes tucked away. Come back to this Phoenix Commandment each time you desire to peel back the layers and remember the most powerful version of yourself.

Phoenix Commandment

"Brilliant Phoenix light, as a direct expression of the Divine, I ask for boldness and courage. I ask that I be able to break free of any energy patterns, disease, beliefs, misperceptions, limited ideas, ancient thought patterns, past-life thought patterns, and old coding that may be holding me back from accessing my highest potential. I ask that all of my cells, thoughts, emotions, and actions shift and rearrange so that the strongest, boldest, most authentic and aligned version of my powerful self may show up in everyday life. I am ready to own my magic in every realm, and I choose to see what I am capable of and what my highest potential and expression are designed to be. Allow me to be, express, and show up in the way that the Maker has created me. Let thy will be done."

Phoenix Mantras

Pick or create a Phoenix mantra to focus on for the day, the week, or the month. You may want to have it displayed on your phone or written on an index card that you can look at often. You may want to say the mantra to yourself in the mirror, repeat it while on a walk, or listen to an audio recording of yourself saying the mantra over and over again. Your voice is one of the most powerful things you can hear, and it can further enhance the effectiveness of the mantra. You can come up with your own Phoenix mantra, or choose one from the following list:

- I am powerful and capable as I am.
- Solutions and answers just come to me.
- I get to be bold and take up space.
- Creation flows through my voice, and I get to be heard.
- My words create.
- My actions create.
- My desires are valuable.
- My desires are guiding me step-by-step.
- People love and accept me as I am.
- I give myself permission to be wildly free.

Use your mantra when you need to feel uplifted and inspired. You may find yourself coming back to these mantras in a month (or even a year), only to find that the mantras have a new layer of meaning for you at that time. As you continue to play with each new thought over time, there will be a moment when the thought becomes a belief, fully accepted by you. Watch as you evolve and grow into a whole new way of being.

Phoenix Ascension Prompts

It's time for some magical self-exploration. Prior to reflecting on these prompts, take a moment to create a sacred space or sit in front of your altar. Setting up your sacred space with flowers, candlelight, and tea or another beverage always adds energy and light to your intention field. The more energy you put into this, the more powerful it will be for you.

Then, connect with the deepest, most intimate parts of yourself. Set the intention of allowing your most wild, actualized self to flow through you—the part of you that is creative, musical, and expressive. Also allow who you desire to be to flow through you as you reflect on these prompts. You may discover a few things about yourself you did not know before, so take the time to really revel in these expressions of yourself.

Connect with your Phoenix self as you reflect on the following questions:

1. If you were free to create your life exactly the way you want it to be, what would that look like? Imagine you had all the money, all the resources, and all of the love and support that you need. What does this world look like for you?

2. If you were to say all the things that you want to say, what would that feel like? What are the powerful conversations that you would allow yourself to have right now?

3. If you completely allowed yourself to take the actions that you want to take, what would they be? What would you eat? Where would you shop? What would you do? How would you spend your day?

4. What are your strategies to protect your own energy? When someone disagrees with you, how can you respect them while remaining firmly in your own energy and your own beliefs? What needs to happen in order for you to continue to create your life by following your own desires?

Channeled Message from the Phoenix

"You are never too much. You are here to be gorgeous, vibrant, and beautiful, and you get to take up space. Be all of yourself."

—Phoenix

Chapter Four
The Dragon

❀

A bird does not sing because it has an answer.
It sings because it has a song.
—CHINESE PROVERB

Whoosh! A puff of smoke rises from a cave, where the magnificent Dragon and all his treasures reside. The Asian Dragon is an enchanting being, with jewels for eyes and powerful magic that can carry his enormous body through the air.

Although there are many dragons from all around the world, each with very different magical traits, in this chapter we will be connecting with Chinese Dragons. These regal, elemental beings represent prosperity, wisdom, and protection.

When we welcome Dragon energy into our lives, new beginnings and possibilities will start to form, and we will have the courage to take risks and say yes. Dragons are protectors and guardians, and they will always help us find the confidence we need to experience and fulfill our life purpose. They imbue us with the power to take action even when we are afraid.

In art and legendary stories, the Chinese Dragon is serpentine, has short legs, and has three to five toes, depending on the breed. Dragons also have thick scales, long whiskers, and luxe furs around the ankles, neck, and tail. They are both reptilian and mammalian. These Dragons do not have wings, but they have the ability to glide through the air as if they are flying. Many of the Dragons from China are depicted with a large pearl between the paw and the jaws. There is an important insignia design called the Dragon Disk found during the Qing (formerly known as Ching) dynasty, worn by a prince.[3]

Dragon Magic

Dragon magic is a portal to extraordinary power. It is one of the most mystical types of magic we have available to us at this time. The medicine of the Dragon transforms us in ways we may never fully comprehend. Even the imagery of the Dragon—available to us in a world where we cannot see actual dragons—shows us the magic of this portal: it is a magic that is so powerful, it has

---

3. Hayes, *The Chinese Dragon*, 21.

slipped into our dimension, and the simple acts of looking at and researching the Dragon open additional portals of possibilities to all aspects of ourselves.

The appearance of the Dragon in so many ancient cultures also reminds us there is more to this world than we currently know or understand, and that there may be aspects of it yet to be seen and discovered. Even people who say they are not into magic find themselves drawn to the Dragon. Part of the mystery of life and existence is that we are not meant to know everything, and if we try to think or believe we do, we will always limit our experiences within our own lives. The fun is in the mystery of it all! Dragon magic is a profound validation of this.

The Dragon awakens our imagination so that we stretch and expand our definitions of life and reality. The very existence of the Dragon encourages us to dream bigger and to be braver. Dragon magic also urges us to remember how capable we are. Movies depict the Dragon blowing fire and burning down entire towns and cities, reminding each of us that we have the power to protect ourselves.

There is even magic in the Dragon egg. Dragon eggs, like most eggs, are symbolic of creation and life. In addition, the very large size of the Dragon egg represents how much is available for us. Dragon magic connects us to an awareness of expansion and rich possibilities.

Samantha's Dragon Story

Each one of us has a special anecdote about finding our inner power, and this is mine.

Dragons have been protecting me for as long as I can remember. Even as a child riding in the car, I would see Dragons flying and weaving through the clouds, keeping me safe amidst traffic. I would see the flame of golden light coming from their mouths, and I would see them play, dancing back and forth in space. When I moved to Shanghai, China, I was able to see the Dragon with even more clarity. I would feel them swishing and swirling around on the subways, propelling people forward and keeping everyone on the subway safe. They are such beautiful, playful, and majestic beings, and they are so loving in every way.

I moved to Shanghai, China, in the summer of 2005, after graduating from Whittier College with a biochemistry degree. While in China, I studied acupuncture, herbal medicine, and Chinese medicine for over five years. While there were so many beautiful parts about studying there, I felt like there was a big piece that was missing for me personally. I wanted more depth, more spirituality, and I wanted to increase my ability to feel life force pulsing through me and my work. Part of me wanted to continue my studies and finish my degree, but there was this other part of me that knew what I was deeply craving was something wildly different.

One night I meditated on the floor of my living room in my place on Nanjing Xi Lu, one of the hippest streets in Shanghai. As I heard the cars buzzing past me, I quieted my mind and allowed myself to go into the deepest and darkest parts of myself and the Universe. I felt and saw this bright, beaming God light I just knew was the light of creation. In that moment, I had the realization that there was not a single place on the planet that the cosmos was not a part of. I saw this so clearly. I also felt the Dragons protecting me and showing me my new path. I saw myself walking away from the Chinese Medicine University I was attending, and I woke up the next morning knowing exactly what I needed to do.

By this point, I had become very proficient with my Reiki, hypnosis, and Emotional Freedom Techniques practices, which were teachings that I had found and studied outside of university. I knew that I had found a frequency of healing that was faster and more efficient for me than what I had been learning at the Chinese Medicine University, and it was time for me to move on. The feeling of life force that I was craving was being found in mystery schools that were much different than what I had expected. In my healing practice, I could send energy to my clients from ten feet away and observe their bodies adjusting themselves. I knew that I was on to something special, and I really wanted to pursue this new path.

Feeling loved and surrounded by my Dragon protectors, I called my university advisor and let her know I had decided to discontinue my studies. She was so perplexed. She said I only had one more month left, as well as one easy exam. I told her that I understood, however, I was finished there and moving on anyway. There was a fiery Sagittarius energy inside of me that knew this was my truth. Immediately after I got off the phone with her, the bookshelf with all of my Chinese Medicine School books collapsed. It was the only shelf that had Chinese Medicine books on it. I knew it was a sign that I had taken the correct path. I boxed up all of my books and donated them back to the school that same week. I was craving mystery and magic, and I needed to take time to explore a new route for myself. It was essential for my body, mind, and spirit that I take bold and brave new steps to find what was genuinely and powerfully aligned for me. I couldn't logically explain what was happening, but I knew deep inside of my body that this was the right choice for me.

My world metaphysical studies began one night as I was going for my evening walk. I looked up at the moon and the stars and said to myself, *God, Cosmos, if you're real, show me a sign. Show me that all of this matters and that what I'm doing matters. I need to see the truth and the deeper meaning to all of this. All of existence. Show me.* It was as if I learned how to pray directly to the Cosmos for the first time. The next day, as if the Dragons took me on a fast track to new world potentials, I was guided to teacher after teacher. My best friend asked if I had ever been to a channeler. I had never even heard of one at the time, so I went to a little metaphysical shop that was also a school called Frank'n'Sense. Each week they'd invite teachers from all over the world, and I signed myself up for every class, even if the classes were quite expensive for me at the time. My soul was guiding me, and I had to follow its direction. Once this world opened up for me, there was no turning back. I had to keep pursuing what else was available in this magical world.

It took several years for my mom to understand this shift, but it was one of the greatest decisions I have ever made in my life. Even in that moment, as it was happening, I remember saying to myself that I would put this in a book one day, and it would serve as an inspiration for other people to know that they, too, are allowed to walk away from something even if they have been invested in it for a long time. The moment that your soul guides you in a new direction, that is your permission slip to take the leap.

I know if I had given myself permission to tap into my power sooner, I would have made that same decision much earlier. It took me several years to truly listen to my genuine desire, until the Dragon surged so much energy through me that I could finally hear my spirit's ask, and I listened. Trust that the Dragon will catch you every single step of the way. Just ask, and your protector will arrive right on time to be there for you. Supporting you is the Dragon's greatest joy. The Dragon's strength and power is immense, as is yours.

Pamela's Dragon Story

The story of finding my inner magic and being able to fly freely, like the majestic Dragon, started right before I moved to Las Vegas in 2005. This was also the time when I was being called to focus more on my spiritual journey and explore and learn about different healing modalities. It was not until much later I understood what an extremely potent and fulfilling time this was for me. The decisions I made during this time are what got me to where I am right now. If the Dragon had not been with me, I don't know if I would be here writing this book and teaching about magic. Let me tell you why.

I had not planned on moving away from Hawaii. I loved all of my many jobs there, and I had a lot of fun hanging out and partying with my friends in Hawaii. However, my lease was up, and since Hawaii is very pricey, I could not find another place to live that was affordable. With the encouragement of my friends and coworkers, I made the split-second decision to move across the Pacific Ocean to what Hawaiians call "the ninth island": Las Vegas.

Not being able to find a place in Hawaii had been really stressful. I knew that moving to Vegas was the right thing for me, and I knew that I was going to be okay, but it took a lot of Dragon magic for me to make this choice, especially because I only had two weeks to decide on this big transition. With support from my powerful guides, I took aligned action on the messages that I had received. And I have been living in Vegas ever since.

At that time, I was a magical newbie, so taking the leap was extra scary; now I know that following intuitive guidance will always work out in my favor. When I look back, I see that taking that action changed my entire life. When I moved to Vegas, I was randomly called to go to this holistic fair by myself. I had no logical reason for going, but my interest in the fair felt similar to the urge to move to Vegas, so I went. At the fair, I met my first psychic and Reiki mentor, who started me on this magical path. Everything slowly continued to unfold for me over the following years and got me to where I am today. You see, the magic and knowledge I have now was not something I was taught growing up or something I manifested as part of a spiritual awakening. Everything happened step-by-step: I took classes, read books, and learned from amazing mentors throughout the years.

A couple of years after moving to Las Vegas, I found myself having a bit of a breakdown, and I had to call upon my Dragon guide for deeper healing again. I hadn't worked with the Dragon for a while, as life had been very busy, and I hadn't needed to work with him specifically. That day, though, something lit up in me, and I knew that the life that I was living, which included drinking and partying, was not the one I was meant to live. After connecting with my Dragon through a meditation journey, I was given the message to keep going. I reached further and asked for specific guidance as to what I needed to do as part of that process. As I tapped back into the Dragon magic, I realized that no matter what choices I made, I would be protected, and that the wisdom I sought would be shown to me when I chose to live in alignment with who I truly was. To me, this meant I needed to allow myself to explore new opportunities and put myself out there in the world if I wanted to create a new life.

With that wisdom always in the back of my mind, I kept trying new things, including getting certifications for healing modalities and learning how to build a business online. I began to trust every step of the beautiful and supportive way my journey was unfolding. I don't think I made the choice to stop partying—it just happened. I was no longer aligned with that version of myself because I was so focused on my true self and my spiritual development.

Since then, I have returned to Dragon magic as needed, and always with the same great results. Now, I embody what I teach and live my magic daily, and I know that Dragon magic can lead anyone who asks to a life of fulfillment.

Setting Up Your Dragon Altar

Your Dragon altar is a powerful space to build up and foster magnetism and protection. It is a sacred container that holds your radiant energy and charisma. The Dragon altar has wisdom floating around in the air, ready for you to capture and embody.

Here are some tools related to Dragon energy that you can use to decorate your altar. These suggestions were guided by Dragon in a meditative channeling that we performed for this book. Feel free to add tools that are familiar to you or any others we have discussed. Always remember the energy of the Dragon is majestic, decisive, and commanding.

Dragon Crystals
Ruby
Pyrite
Emerald

Dragon Colors
Red
Gold
White

Dragon Symbols
Fire
Jewelry
Pearls

Dragon Food Offerings
Dragons aren't picky—anything you have would work. They do have a sweet tooth, though!
Honey cakes
Dark chocolate
Cookies
Pie
Cider

Dragon Tarot Cards
The Magician
The Hierophant
The Emperor

Create a ceremony to honor the Dragon daily. Dragons love gold and fire, so if you can light a candle or drop some gold coins (chocolate gold coins will do) onto your altar, they would appreciate the offerings. Make sure that when you greet your Dragon, you state your intentions or mantras with power—they love to grant wishes that are spoken in a commanding voice. To embody the energy of the Dragon, lie down on the ground and imagine that you are swimming in a pile of gold, stretching your arms out like they are wings.

After you have finished setting up your potent Dragon altar, activate the altar by calling in your Dragon guide using the instructions in the next section.

Meeting Your Dragon Guide

Take a few deep breaths. Settle your body and your mind. Find yourself in your own magical space. It is time to meet your Dragon guardians. Feel a level of cheerfulness as you sink into meditation.

White and gold light enters the room. It holds you sweetly, and you see yourself cozy underneath the mandarin tree. A soft swoosh of wind blows across your face, and you hear rustling leaves. Two Dragon protector guides have entered. Their smooth scales and fluffy fur swirl around you, and you feel embraced by their immense power, love, and charm. They have been eager to introduce themselves to you. The Dragons have been here with you your entire life, playing in the background. They have been patiently waiting for you to invite them in.

The Dragons are youthful in appearance, but majestic wisdom beams as a result of their ancient age. The brightness that emanates from them shows how lighthearted they are, and that all matter becomes light again, even if we have to first wade through some deep, dark moments. You feel the hair on your body rise as the Dragons swish and swirl past you. The love they beam is such a high frequency, it is not of this world.

The Golden Dragon invites you to sit on his back, while the White Dragon waves to follow him. You jump on the back of the Golden Dragon, who follows the White Dragon, as they take to the sky. Together, you soar through the clouds and move through the golden veil between this Universe and the next.

The Golden Dragon has flown you into another world. As you move through layers of opaque rainbow light, you finally arrive in the World of the Dragons. It is filled with luscious green meadows, rainbows, and waterfalls. Light sparkles over the land. You see many dragons in this enchanted world. You also see the Great Golden Temple of Light. The Golden and White Dragons fly you directly to temple's palace.

When you land, you see that there is a gorgeous banquet waiting for you. Here are all of your Dragon guides and protectors, waiting to meet you and connect. There is the Bronze Dragon and other Dragons of various colors, all with their own unique wisdom, ready to awaken your senses.

You feel the warmth of family and the immense love of the Dragons. They invite you to eat with them. As you eat, drink, and laugh, you notice how beautifully prepared all the food is. The colors and the fragrance make your entire body come to life. Each Dragon then presents you with a gift, a potion, or an elixir; this is something that you can take in while speaking with the Dragons.

The Sky Blue Dragon gives you the elixir of life. This potion will awaken your senses and help you see the lushness that the Dragons feel and see. The colors in your Universe will brighten.

The Bronze Dragon gifts you with the magic of being recognized for your brilliance. "It's safe to be seen, and to be bright for no reason at all," he says, smiling at you.

The Golden Dragon gives you the potion of vision. This will support you in both seeing and feeling love, even when it feels hard to do so. Love is always present, and this sunshine potion will remind you of that.

The White Dragon gifts you a soft silk scarf. This is the gift of the softness of the feminine. Softness and gentleness will protect you when you least expect it.

Dragons upon Dragons come in with unique gifts, showering you with all of the love of the Universe. Tears may stream down your face as you feel the immense magic emanating from your Dragon protector guides. You see that they have all been overflowing with abundant gifts, just waiting to shower you in presents.

Each Dragon kisses you on the forehead as a way of sealing in all of the gifts. They let you know that you are welcome to come back and receive magical upgrades at any time, and that you're welcome to just visit their land too. They joyously share that they are as close to you as the blink of an eye. The moment you think of their presence, you have direct access to them. You feel wrapped up in their love, an immensely powerful, out-of-this-world kind of love. Intuitively, your hands find their way over your heart, and you fully embrace this new energetic frequency.

You tug on the fur of the Golden Dragon and climb on his back once more. Together with the White Dragon, you are flown back through the opaque rainbow light, into your Universe and your home space. The Dragons embrace you in warm hugs and blow golden air into your lungs. They tell you they are with you always, and you're welcome to ask them for a boost of power or magic at any time. They will always be your allies, powerfully standing by your side. You know that you will never be the same.

As you fly back into your body, you notice the rise and fall of your chest with your breath. Feel the warmth in your fingertips and toes. Notice the sensation of blood flowing through your body. There is an inner peace and happiness that gently stirs within you. A new awareness that you are not alone and that you are so deeply held and magically loved by the Dragons makes you feel a cocoon of love. You were always loved, sweet one. You are incredibly cherished and wonderfully cared for by all of creation, and now that magic is even more strongly anchored within you.

Flying Dragon Ritual

Dragons from the East glide powerfully through the air without wings. They remind us that it is not about what you have on the outside—it is what you cultivate on the inside that makes a difference. This Flying Dragon Ritual will unlock hidden superpowers that can help you accomplish your goals. What you are activating is wisdom, energy, and magic that can guide you on your way to your success. Remember, everything you are looking for externally is already present internally. The Dragons will help you unlock your innate gifts.

Before you start this ritual, think about a question that you would like to have answered. Focus on one question at a time; you can always do this ritual multiple times with different questions. To best serve you on your magical journey, do not ask the Dragons yes or no questions. Instead, ask empowering questions such as "What inspired actions can I take to reach my goals?" or "How can I shift or change to achieve my intentions?"

To prep for the ritual, you will first need to connect with your Dragon guide using the meditation in the previous section of this chapter. Afterward, gather these magical tools:

A picture of you

White yarn or string

White candle

A treasure or piece of jewelry that you can wear or hold on to daily

Lighter or matches

Envelope that will fit your photo and the treasure

Pen

Cleanse your sacred space and Dragon altar with an herbal wand or spray and set up your magical tools for the ritual. Make sure you are in a place where you won't be disturbed for the duration of your ritual. Your ritual can be as long as you want, depending on the time you want to stay in the energy of the Dragon and the size of your candle.

1. Take the photo of you and wrap it with white yarn, until it is completely covered. As you are wrapping the photo, ask your empowered question. Think of it or ask it out loud—whatever feels best for you.

2. When the photo is completely covered, tie off the yarn or tuck it underneath the other yarn so that it stays put.

3. As you reflect on your question, think of a power word that you would like to invoke. This should be an energy you would like to call in to help you accomplish your mission. It can be something as simple as *wisdom* or *abundance*. One of our favorite words to embody is *easy*. Whichever word you choose, write it on the envelope.

4. Put the yarn-covered photo inside the envelope. Also add your chosen treasure, then seal the envelope. Hold the envelope to your heart and imagine a golden light beaming into it as you activate your power word and exchange energies. See this golden light go into your heart space as you breathe in, and imagine the light going into the envelope as you breathe out. Do this as many times as you like. When you are finished, put the envelope in front of the candle on your altar.

5. Light your candle and say, "Dragon of the East, come to me. I ask you [question], and I ask you to activate the

magic and power within me to call in [intention]. Thank you, thank you, thank you. And so it is."

6. Put your palms together in prayer position. Hold them over your heart and imagine the worst possible outcome of your goal. Really lean into it. Then, imagine a breath of fire from the Dragons burning it up. Next, imagine your ideal outcome. Let your Dragon guide you to the perfect future. Remember every single detail of what you are experiencing, including what you are seeing, hearing, and feeling. When you are done visualizing your inevitable future, open your eyes and write it down.

7. Your spell will be complete when the candle is finished burning. Make sure you do not leave an open flame unattended. During this time, your connection to the Dragon will be amplified. Use this opportunity to journal, and allow messages from your core self and your intuition to inspire guidance or instructions that can help you manifest your intention.

When the candle has finished burning, open the envelope and take out your two items. Unwrap the yarn from your photo and feel energy expanding with each unraveling. The photo is a reminder that you are the creator, and you have the answers to everything you seek. Put this photo on your Dragon altar or under your pillow until you have achieved your goal, or until you are ready for a new goal. Take the treasure and keep it with you for luck, guidance, and blessings. You will find that opportunities show up in the most unexpected ways. Whenever you like, you can recharge the treasure on your Dragon altar, or you can infuse it with new magic for another goal once you are done with this work.

Sacred Code Activations

The Dragon is by your side to speed up and amplify the power of your energy and your creations. In those moments when you feel small and unseen, call upon the Dragon. The Dragon will power up your love, your energy, and your light. The goodness inside of you will be amplified and felt by those around you so that you can create the impact you desire and be acknowledged for your true worth. Use the Dragon Commandment to amplify your power. Know that the love of the Dragon is immense, and this energy radiates ancestrally and into future timelines.

Dragon Commandment

"Activating Dragon power, as a direct expression of the Divine, I ask to access unimaginable power and strength in my being. I choose to use this power to bring light and goodness into my world and into the world of others. I ask to dissolve and break free of any thoughts that distort my understanding of pure and enlightened power. I ask for new insight and understanding to be downloaded in a way that creates win-win situations. I call upon my deepest bravery and my boldest courage from all the realms. I accept my divine light and my divine gift to create power and amplify power in a positive way that generates and creates goodness for all. I ask for wisdom to wisely use this power for the creation of light in all areas of my Universe and the Universe of others."

Dragon Mantras

Your voice is one of the most powerful instruments of creation that you own. As you say new words and new phrases to yourself over and over again, you begin to create new thought patterns.

These new thought patterns begin to reshape the neural connections in your brain. As you train yourself to have higher-frequency thoughts, you begin to create higher-frequency experiences in your Universe. Create a recording of you saying these phrases to yourself. Play them over and over again until together they become your new reality.

- I accept and enjoy the power within me.
- It is safe for me to be powerful and to trust my inner power.
- My power benefits me and the people around me.
- I get to stay in my power, even when I am around other powerful people.
- My style of power is unique to me.
- My power gets to be used to create really amazing things in my life and in the lives of others.
- I feel safe and comfortable with my power.
- I choose to use the power that surges through me wisely and with love.
- The power that runs through me is a gift from the Universe, and I fully accept it.
- The things that I create are powerful.

Dragon Ascension Prompts

It's time to get cozy and dive deep into your inner world. Grab your favorite beverage, and perhaps set some flowers or crystals by your side. If there is something powerful that you'd like to be reminded of, feel free to place a token of this awareness on your altar so that the energy can be amplified.

Enter a space where you get to deeply connect with the most intimate parts of yourself. This is a moment between you, the

Creator, and your Dragon guardians. The more intentional you are with these ascension prompts, the more powerful they will be. You may discover something new about yourself. If a question that is not written here pops into your consciousness, let yourself answer it. Trust the free-flowing connection between you and Spirit. You are always guided in each and every moment.

1. If you knew that your power would do good, and that you were allowed to express it in your own way, how would you use your power?

2. How did you see your mom, dad, teachers or adults in your life use power when you were growing up? What examples serve you? What stories and examples do not serve you? How are you able to create your own blissful way of using your power?

3. If you truly believed in your own power, what would you create?

4. If you truly believed in your own power, what would you step away from?

5. If you truly believed in your own power, what would you ask the Universe to send you?

Channeled Message from the Dragon

"By the Imperial Seal of the Universe, you are and always have been granted the gift of enlightened power. Your power is meant to be used and expressed uniquely by you for your pure pleasure. You are free to trust that your power will be used for good in the world and that we will be behind you, guiding you, every step of the way."

—DRAGON

Chapter Five
The Money Frog

❁

The emperor is rich, but he cannot buy one extra year.
—Chinese Proverb

The Money Frog is always on the path to wealth. With three powerful legs, this magical being can hop into the future and collapse time to help us achieve our goals. The Money Frog's three legs represent the past, present, and future. This frog loves to be in the energy of prosperity and will reward those that vibrate at the same frequency. When you are attuned to the energy of the Money Frog, possibilities and opportunities will appear right in front of you. These possibilities and opportunities, more impressive than you could ever imagine, can lead to an abundance of money. You might have to take a few jumps to get there, but it will be worth it in the end.

A Chinese myth that our grandparents and parents told us when we were growing up says that if someone sees a toad hopping near a home or business on a full moon, it means that person will have a windfall of success and good luck. However, our favorite story about the Money Frog is that it is one of the animal companions of the immortals (another name for God or Goddess in Chinese). In this way, the Money Frog bestows financial wealth to the home.

In Japan, you will find plenty of frog coin purses for sale. In Japanese, the word *Kaeru* has a double meaning: it can mean to return home, but it also means "frog." Therefore, the belief is that by carrying money in a frog coin purse, the money is being told to return home fast, and with some friends! The Money Frog is definitely a fun symbol and a good luck charm for all.

Unsurprisingly, the Money Frog, also known as the prosperity toad, *Jin Chan*, is a popular feng shui symbol. Feng shui is a Chinese system that ensures good energetic flow and invites prosperity into a space. It is a tool that many people in Asian cultures utilize to attract abundance, luck, and health, though it is used by other cultures as well. (We will talk more about feng shui in chapter 11.) With that being said, there are a few things a Money Frog figurine must have in order to garner good fortune for a home. First, the Money Frog must have a coin in its mouth and be elevated; it is usually sitting on a pile of coins, gold, or money. Second, the Money Frog must have a bit of the color red on it or be sitting on top of something red, such as a red envelope, in order to be activated; you can choose any red item that resonates with you. It is also advised that the Money Frog be placed in the far-left corner of the room or home, which is the prosperity corner in feng shui. This will encourage the Money Frog to bring in more wealth. Keep in mind that the Money Frog is never to be placed in a bathroom, bedroom, or kitchen.

One thing to note is that most people think wanting and having more money is related to greed, which, most of the time, really is just illustrating their own past programming from other people or events. This mindset can result in keeping abundance away. The truth is, money does not make you into anything—rather, it enhances who you are. For example, if you are a greedy person, then you will become greedier. If you are a compassionate, caring person, then money will amplify that. If you manifest a massive amount of money after connecting with the Money Frog, you will receive different reactions from people. Friends and family might support you and celebrate you, or they may have negative feedback for you. Don't take jealous reactions of others to heart; this is likely a reaction caused by their own personal issues around money, or even subconscious past programming.

To protect yourself, ask the Money Frog to shield you in a golden light that only allows positive energies to flow through to you. You do not need to share information about your wealth with the public, either—you can keep it to yourself, or perhaps find a new group of people who have an abundance mindset like you do. Money is a measurement of our success and sometimes even a reflection of our spiritual growth. If you have begun the next stage of your magical journey, sometimes you have to leave others behind who do not support where you want to go. Send everyone loving energy and Money Frog magic, and then move on.

Money Frog Magic

Money Frog magic represents the powerful leaps of faith that live within each of us. These cosmic sparks launch us toward expansion and saying yes to things that free us from limitations and societal constructs. This energy is the inner power that guides us to open doors to new possibilities and potentials. It's also the quiet voice (sometimes the loud voice!) inside us encouraging us to take risks and trust that the Universe will catch us. The Money Frog is a reminder that we are safe and guided every single step of the way, and that expansion and creation are always available to us.

This leap-of-faith energy is an innate wisdom inside of us that understands the power of pleasure, play, and trust. This is the magic of the Money Frog. Leaping from one mystical moment to the next, he inspires spontaneity and creativity. It is in joyful and courageous moments that strokes of genius arise within us. The Money Frog is present when the call to create is so much louder than the fear of failing.

Society has programmed us to play it safe and to do the same routines over and over again, even though this often stifles our spirit and slows down our evolution. The Money Frog is here to remind us that there are more inspirational ways of living as we take courageous leaps of faith to follow our heart. All of creation is available to us. Trusting our inner guidance leads to an even more luscious and abundant version of life than we can imagine. The Universe wants all of us to delight in play and pleasure.

The Money Frog reminds us we have a spiritual intuition built into our very existence. As we fine-tune our subtle senses and learn to listen to inner exclaims of joy, we feel and see that this guidance and intuition has been available for us every single step of the way. It may not be logical at all times, but this guidance is nudging us toward an even more joyful and playful reality. Things are not always what they appear to be. By learning to listen to the innate wisdom of the body, we will find that riches abound, and they are available now! This is the power of the Money Frog.

Samantha's Money Frog Story

Money used to be a sticky subject in my family. I saw the topic of money create so much stress in my family, resulting in many disempowering decisions, that I dedicated several years of my life to the study of wealth and opulence so I could liberate myself and others from this energetic entanglement. I believe this is why I was inspired to become an opulence coach and teach people about the law of increasing abundance and how to strengthen their life force energy to create more money. But that is not to say that it has always been easy.

My toughest times financially were the two years after I moved back to Vancouver, Washington, from Shanghai, China. In 2011, I had moved back home to be with my family, and it felt like I had to restart my business completely. While living in Shanghai, I had had a fully booked, successful practice where I shared Reiki, Emotional Freedom Techniques, hypnosis, and acupuncture services. I had even been featured in a couple of magazines and found myself giving talks to crowds of up to three thousand people. These situations seemed to just find me. I was able to easily make six thousand to eight thousand dollars per month, which was a huge achievement for me at the time.

However, when I went back to Washington, I really struggled. I went back to charging twenty dollars a session and still had hardly any bookings. It's as if when I moved back to my hometown, all of my old, limiting financial beliefs came rushing back in to remind me where I came from. I felt so much fear and anxiety around the topic of money all the time. I knew I needed change, and luckily, the Money Frog was there to guide me.

I was ready to take my business to the next level, so I rented a small space to see clients out of a yoga studio. Renting a space already felt outside of my comfort zone, yet the Money Frog assured me it would be the best course of action. On my first day in that space, I made one thousand dollars. I was astonished!

A few months into renting, I was lucky enough to have the Money Frog jump into my awareness again, when I was guided to my very first money coach. I was online watching something not at all related to money. Suddenly, I was guided to a webinar on the seven chakras and money. Everything the presenter talked about resonated with me completely. Prior to this, it never occurred to me that money could be an energy or that it was connected to our emotional well-being as well. I decided I wanted to work with this coach, but I had to put my payment for her services on a credit card, which felt like a huge leap of faith. It was also one of the best decisions of my life.

Money Frog leaps may not make logical sense in the moment, but the leap feels so joyful that we know it is essential. It can be a bit scary to take the risks we are guided to take, but at the same time, it will all feel so right. I invested over three thousand dollars on my first money coach. That was the most I had ever spent on a course or a coach at any time. But then, in the next two weeks, I made six thousand dollars. I couldn't believe it! Things were shifting as I did deeper work around my issues with money. I had no idea I had so many emotions bottled up around money. I began using strategies that helped me energetically, including Emotional Freedom Techniques, to release the emotions surrounding my most traumatic money memories.

My next Money Frog leap of faith was when I was trying to sell my first six-month coaching program, which cost $15,500. I was suddenly strongly guided to listen to the classic book *Think and Grow Rich* by Napoleon Hill. I listened to the entire Audible in two days! Then, I listened to *The Science of Getting Rich* by Wallace D. Wattles. One week later, I made the $15,500 sale. This then led to a $20,664 sale and, not long after, my first month earning fifty thousand dollars. What was so crazy was that all of it was simply the result of changing my internal belief system. Before, I didn't believe I could earn this kind of money, and I didn't believe I was worthy of receiving it. It took me a very long time to relax my mind enough to simply let money flow in, and to allow myself to receive it.

I realized that receiving this amount of money was a frequency, a relaxed way of thinking and feeling in which I was fully connected to the support of the Universe. I also came to understand that parts of me had been addicted to drama and suffering because that was all I had known. I had to continuously recondition myself that it was safe to feel fully relaxed and confident in myself.

My most extraordinary money manifestation happened when a close family member came to visit me in Santa Barbara, California. I decided to step away from my business entirely during that time and only focus on her. I took her to parties and brunches and made her salt baths and bubble baths. I took her to my favorite chiropractor, and we went on beach walks. All the while, in the back of my mind, I kept saying to myself, *Money is on its way.* I wasn't doing my normal marketing or advertising, so I wasn't even sure how new clients would find me during that time. Yet, I kept repeating that thought: *Money is on its way.* That week, $5,300 simply appeared in my checking account. The following month, $8,300 appeared in my account. I tried to track these deposits to determine where this money came from, but it looked like *I* had deposited these amounts, and I knew I definitely had not. I could not trace them!

I realized these deposits were the result of the Money Frog opening up new portals for me. This is the reality we live in, and it is not as rigid or as black-and-white as we may think it is. When we relax our minds and our bodies, we allow miracles to flow to us. The strongest thought wins. The Universe wants to shower us with abundance. This is the gift of the Money Frog: once you finally take the leap, prosperity awaits!

Pamela's Money Frog Story

This is a fun story about how my friends and I worked with the Money Frog during a day at the beach.

One of the times I went back to Hawaii to visit my friends, we decided to do a prosperity ritual. Each of my friends was either looking for a new job, a raise, or more money in general. So, we circled together on Waikiki Beach and laid out a beautiful floral centerpiece. We surrounded the flowers with money, incense, and coins, and then we set a golden Money Frog right in the center.

We sat around the abundance altar that we had created and I opened space, calling in our guides, teachers, the five Chinese elements, and of course, the Money Frog. Then, we each said what it was that we wanted to call in. I had asked my friends to specifically write the amount of money that they wanted to manifest and to speak as if it had already happened, exactly like the methods we share in this book. Then all of my friends took turns touching the Money Frog's head for gratitude and good luck—there wasn't really a reason for doing this other than that we felt guided to.

My friends and I didn't win the lottery or anything that day, but a few weeks later, all of us begin to experience increases in prosperity and our finances. A couple of my friends got the jobs that they wanted, which paid even more than they had asked for. One of my friends was able to easily sell her home for cash. Another won a lot of money during a two-week streak of playing poker. In my case, right when I got back from Hawaii, I had a big money-making week at work.

Money likes the frequency of play, and that's what we did that day. It wasn't a serious ritual nor one that took a long time. Instead, my friends and I tuned in to what we desired, trusted our intuition to guide us, did what felt good, and had a lot of fun at the beach. When working with the Money Frog, if you feel called to do something, always follow your heart and do it! The most important thing you can do is stay detached from the outcome. My friends and I did not obsess over what we asked for that day. Instead, we released our desires and let the Money Frog work. The attitude you should adopt is "My life is amazing, and wouldn't it be even more amazing if I had more wealth?" instead of "I need money" (even if you really do). Remember, you will attract what you focus on. So, focus on fun, laughter, joy, and feeling abundant. Turn your attention to having a good time and go with the flow. When you do, money miracles will occur.

Setting Up Your Money Frog Altar

Your Money Frog altar will create beautiful wealth for you and your loved ones. Keep in mind that, according to feng shui, the placement of the Money Frog altar is very important. To invite abundance into your home, place your Money Frog altar close to the front door, but not directly in line with the door. Another important element of this altar is elevating your Money Frog figurine and placing a coin in its mouth. Doing so will activate the Money Frog to attract wealth and health. Also, make sure that your Money Frog is kept clean, and that you tend to it often.

If you want to increase your prosperity quickly, you could decide to have three, six, or nine Money Frog figurines, as these are all lucky feng shui numbers. You could place one on the main altar by the front door, another in the wealth corner of the home (which is the far-left corner), and one at the far-left corner of your desk.

Make sure that the Money Frog figurine is facing in toward the home in order to create money inside of the house. Some traditions have the Money Frog facing toward the front door during the day so that the Money Frog will go out in order to bring money home; at night, you would turn the Money Frog in so that it is facing the home. Use your intuition to determine which method feels best for you.

Here are some tools related to Money Frog energy that you can use to decorate your altar. These suggestions were guided by Money Frog in a meditative channeling that we performed for this book. Feel free to add tools that are familiar to you or any others we have discussed. Always remember the energy of the Money Frog is freedom, joy, and abundance.

Money Frog Crystals
Green aventurine
Peridot
Jade

Money Frog Colors
Gold
Red
Bronze

Money Frog Symbols
Money
Coins
Ingot (block of gold or silver in an oblong shape)

Money Frog Food Offerings
Peach
Orange
Cabbage

Money Frog Tarot Cards
Wheel of Fortune
The World
The Sun

Create a ceremony to honor the Money Frog daily. It can be as simple as greeting your Money Frog every morning, sharing what you would like to call in for the day, lighting a candle, and even giving them a little pat or high five. You can recite commands, affirmations, and mantras in front of your altar. If you want to get fancy, you can embody the Money Frog and hop around the room, as if you are jumping into your abundance. Really allow yourself to feel the energy of that.

After you have finished setting up your prosperous Money Frog altar, activate the altar by calling in your Money Frog guide using the instructions in the next section.

Meeting Your Money Frog Guide

The Money Frog guide is always ready and excited to bring you riches from mystical and mysterious places. Call upon the Money Frog guide when you're wanting to create something new in your world and are desiring abundance.

Begin by imagining yourself sitting under the fruitful mandarin tree. Notice how bright you feel and how loved you are. Give yourself an ample amount of time to relax and tune in before proceeding with the meditation.

Close your eyes. Imagine yourself on the most gorgeous, vibrant lily pad. As you sit upon this large and luscious lily pad, you notice it is floating on top of shimmering and sparkling water. This water looks and feels different because of the way it glistens. It appears to be a living water that radiates a kind of life force energy. Allow yourself to breathe in the life force from the water.

Feel a cooling and calming sensation flow through your body. A white, gold, and blue light runs up and down your spine. As you sit, relaxed and in tune with yourself, you hear a frog approaching you, closer and closer. As the sound gets louder, you can feel waves of energy running through your body. This energy is clearing your senses and relieving your body of layers of stress. The sound of the frog also begins to heal you, and subtle relaxation washes over your body.

The frog leaps over to you and turns into a giant Money Frog. He motions for you to hop on his back, then swiftly carries you off, taking you through the portals of the Universe and then through all of your previous timelines. You begin to see that all of the times you thought you had wasted money, all of that money was actually collected and is still available for you. The money had never been spent, only circulated. You begin to see all of the beauty, power, and magic that this circulation of money you were a part of created.

Quickly, the Money Frog carries you to your current world. He shows you money that is readily available to you right now. Suddenly, solutions and new ways of feeling and thinking open up for you. He communicates that it is important for you to continue to relax your mind, and that more solutions may come to you in a dream or other means throughout the week.

Leaping through time and space, the Money Frog now takes you to your future. Moving very quickly, through a vortex of light, he shows you large heaps of money that are waiting for you. He nudges at a spot on your forehead, near your third eye. Through a thought transmission, he shows you it's your perspective that allows you to open the portals to all of the magical wealth available to you. The Money Frog then shows you that the riches are simply a thought, and you are able to access this powerful world now.

As new sensations flood your system and your body quickly organizes the information, you settle into a deeper peace and a greater level of acceptance for yourself and all of creation. A part of you is reminded of the richness of the fabric of creation. The Money Frog gifts you a golden coin that has a ruby-red gem in the middle. He shares with you that this level of luck, money, and prosperity lives inside of you, and you can access it any time.

The Money frog leaps away and you find yourself back on the green lily pad. The water around you fades as you return back to your room and your body. Take three long deep breaths and allow yourself to return. Gently move your fingertips and toes, and feel a sense of grounding as a new connection to the Money Frog has been firmly established. Hopefully, you leave the meditation excited to see how things unfold after connecting to your Money Frog guide. In the days ahead, be sure to write down any mystical money experiences, no matter how small. The more positive evidence you gather, the clearer and stronger your connection to the Money Frog will become.

Money Frog Prosperity Ritual

The Money Frog would like to give you a warning, and that is that when you perform this ritual, you can expect a massive up-leveling of your finances, so get ready for some riches! Before you start working with the Money Frog, set an intention that wealth will always come to you in the highest and best ways for you. Also, always be very clear about exactly how much money you are calling in, and where this money is going. Where will you spend the beautiful money you are calling in?

Know that there are no "right" or "wrong" money intentions. You can spend your money on big purchases, like a house or vacation, or you can ask the Money Frog to bring in wealth for a designer purse or more clothing. Your money should make you happy and support you on your life's journey. Whatever you desire is perfect, and you were destined for it.

To prep for the ritual, you will first need to connect with your Money Frog guide using the meditation in the previous section of this chapter. Afterward, gather these magical tools:

Gold Money Frog figurine (make sure it has a coin in its mouth)

Five green candles

Five candleholders

A stack of money in the largest denominations you have

Coins

Salt, any kind

Basil

Bowl

Money crystals (any crystals that are green or gold)

Small piece of paper

Pen or pencil

Lighter or matches

Cleanse your sacred space and Money Frog altar with an herbal wand or spray and set up your magical tools for the ritual. Make sure you are in a place where you won't be disturbed for the duration of your ritual. Your ritual can be as long as you want, depending on the time you want to stay in the energy of the Money Frog and the size of your candles.

1. Sit in front of your Money Frog altar and visualize yourself achieving your goals and making that money. Next, write down your intention on the piece of paper as if it has already happened. For example: "I am so thankful to have $50,000 or more in my bank account, and I accept this, or something better. And so it is. Thank you." Make sure to incorporate gratitude to amplify the power of the intention.

2. Set your intention paper in the bowl and cover it with salt and basil. Then fill the bowl with your Money Frog, crystals, coins, and some rolled-up bills from the stack of cash. If you want to add more money symbols, feel free to do so.

3. Surround the bowl with the rest of the bills, creating a circle of money around your Money Frog.

4. Arrange the five candles in a larger circle, one that surrounds around everything. Alternatively, you could

arrange the candles in a star or any other shape you'd like, as long as it is larger than the circle of bills.

5. When you are ready to activate the Money Frog, light all five candles. As you light each candle, repeat your intention aloud.

6. After all the candles are lit, put your hands over the Money Frog and imagine wealth, money, and riches raining down on you. You can also visualize your intention again.

7. Once lit, do not leave the candles unattended, and make sure they are safe from fire hazards. If you have to leave, snuff (not blow) them out with a snuffer. You can relight the candles when you return, making sure to repeat your intention. Your ritual is finished when all five candles have burned down.

8. Dispose of the candle stubs, wax droppings, and salt in a trash can or bury them. Put your Money Frog back on your altar, where the energy of this ritual will continue to attract abundance into your life. The crystals, coins, and money can also be left on the altar or carried with you. If you feel called to spend the money or give it away, please do so! Sharing the magic can bring good fortune. Just make sure that when you present the bill(s) to someone, the face of the bill is facing them.

Use this prosperity ritual to recharge the abundance in your sacred space whenever you feel like you need a boost of wealth.

Sacred Code Activations

When you need a money miracle, call upon the Money Frog. Our minds tend to overcomplicate things, and our emotions can get entangled into undesirable outcomes—this is when you should call upon the Money Frog's magic. Money Frog will remind you of the joyfulness, the playfulness, and the happiness of life. Money miracles are only seconds, minutes, or moments away, and they are accessed from the current moment. The Money Frog Commandment takes you to the frequency of miracles and activates wealth beyond your wildest dreams.

Money Frog Commandment

"Generous, opulent Money Frog, as a direct expression of the Divine, I ask that you gift me the courage to take the leap to my next level of wealth and abundance. Infuse in me the bountiful energy essential for me to take the leap, adjust my identifications with things that don't serve me in this regard, and adjust my perspective of life so I can see, generate, and create even more wealth in my Universe. I am ready for the changes that are essential for me to be an extraordinary steward of wealthy energy. I understand that more wealth equals more energy, and I am ready and available for this new level of energy to flow through me. Support me in releasing and clearing away any old energetic entanglements of a scarcity mindset from past lives, childhood, or other dimensions of reality that may be currently affecting me. I am ready to take the leap and fully choose and embrace wealth, money, and opulence. Thank you for this incredible and generous transmission of light. May all beings around me feel this level of peace with money and wealth creation."

Money Frog Mantras

The Money Frog is the transmission of joy and ease. This guide is here to remind you that wealth is your natural birthright. It is something that is always available to you when you allow the waterfall of prosperity to flow into your life. As you adjust and fine-tune your beliefs about wealth, more money will find its way to you magically. These Money Frog mantras can help guide you through that process:

- Taking the Spirit-led leap always lands me with more riches.
- I am opening portals to fast wealth that feel light, joyful, and available to me.
- More wealth is flowing to me with peace and ease.
- Money naturally gravitates toward me and finds its way to me in leaps and bounds.
- More wealth than I can even imagine is pouring into my Universe and seems to keep pouring in.
- Three, six, or nine Money Frogs are always eagerly bringing me money from all corners and areas of the Universe.
- My wealth seems to keep growing and growing in mysterious ways.

You may decide to focus on one mantra, or choose a couple to play with throughout the month. Pick mantras that light you up inside and make you feel emotionally elevated. Keep working with these mantras until it feels like you've integrated these new beliefs.

Money Frog Ascension Prompts

Take a few moments to create a sacred space where you will be able to journal. Have your favorite beverage close by and perhaps a small bouquet of flowers. Once you feel comfortable, begin to write in your journal. Respond to these prompts as if you're writing your reality into creation. Send clear signals to the Universe and the Money Frog about your genuine desires. Also pay attention to any new ideas that pop up.

1. What changes do you need to make to your thoughts in order to feel really good about all of the income that is coming into your life now?

2. What are the most miraculous ways you can imagine money leaping into your life right now?

3. How can you practice gratitude and thank the money that is currently in your life?

4. What words would be best to say to yourself to feel even more confident and at ease?

5. If you were to drop all your limiting beliefs about money and view your finances neutrally, what amount of money would you joyfully invite into your life?

6. If you firmly believed in yourself, how much money would you genuinely ask the Universe for, and how would you feel? How can you feel this level of opulence, joy, and gratitude more often?

Channeled Message from the Money Frog

"The world is here for you to play as extravagantly as you want to. Wealth and riches will be provided for you. With a joyful and playful spirit, trust is present, and trust is all that is required for the Universe to deliver its wealth and riches to you."

—MONEY FROG

Part Three
The Ancient Ways, Deities, and Ancestors

Chapter Six
The Golden Ancestors

To forget one's ancestors is to be a brook
without a source, a tree without root.
—Chinese Proverb

Every year, there are traditions and celebrations to honor the cycle of life and death, and to celebrate those who have come before us: the Golden Ancestors. (Golden Ancestors are your ancestors who have already ascended that are no longer attached to their ego personalities. They have healed and gone through training and are ready to help you as a guide.) Some of these celebrations include Halloween, Day of the Dead, and for the Chinese, on July 1, Gates of the Ghosts. While there are many practices and rituals, the one thing everyone agrees on is the honoring of ancestors.

Some of you might be lucky enough to have a family spiritual practice already, or a mentor who has taught you how to honor your Golden Ancestors. For those of you that are hearing about honoring your ancestors for the first time, or just realizing how powerful it is to honor them, you are in the perfect place. Chaweon Koo wrote in her book, *Spell Bound*, that you don't even have to know the names of your ancestors, nor do they have to be recently deceased, for you to work with them in a magical way. And if you were adopted, you can research your home country or even the general region where your blood ancestors came from to tap into that magic.[4]

In our culture, we leave an ancestral altar up at all times and pray to it every day, and we also make some sort of offering like drinks, food, or incense. When praying to the ancestral altar, one can also ask to be blessed in all endeavors and share that they are open to receiving gifts from their ancestors. During special holidays like New Year's, or on ancestors' birthdays, we also light incense for them on the altar. If family is visiting, or if we are visiting family who also have an ancestral altar, greeting the ancestors by lighting incense and saying hello would be proper in our tradition. It is respectful to clean the altar, especially if it gets messy with ashes or if there is a lot of dust. Have set times to clean your altar, for it is a ritual of honoring your ancestors.

---

4. Koo, *Spell Bound*, 23.

In this chapter, you will be given all the tools and guidance you need to start your own ancestral spiritual practice. There are massive benefits to cultivating a connection with Golden Ancestors, and the most powerful magic we can receive from them is to access the gifts hidden within our lineage, gifts that have already been experienced and refined by them. Keep in mind that it is not the personalities of our ancestors that we are connecting with. Rather, we are connecting with their already enlightened and evolved selves: Golden Ancestors.

After our ancestors pass, they go into soul training in the other world and evolve with new knowledge. All ancestors that pass go through this kind of soul training. Sometimes, when mediums are connecting to ancestors, they are connecting to soul fragments or the personality aspects of certain ancestors that may have chosen not to leave the earthly plane yet. Those are aspects of the personality that are still attached to the earthly realm. These are just energy packets and not the full soul of the departed. The full souls of the ancestors have already ascended and returned back to Source for healing and training. However, personality traits and energy packets can still be left in the earthly plane. We are not connecting to those aspects of the ancestors—we are connecting to the whole soul of the ancestor who has already healed from this lifetime and gone through light training.

These Golden Ancestors also have access to the gifts within your ancestral DNA and know how to support you in unlocking this wisdom. This may include working with magic, healing modalities, and manifestation. But working with Golden Ancestors is not only about healing past-life trauma, which is what many healers focus on; we can work with them on anything we need help with in our lives. Connecting to your Golden Ancestors is very easy, similar to calling upon your spirit guides or angels. All you have to do is get centered and ask for their support.

The Meeting Your Golden Ancestors Guide section of this chapter will help you attune to their energies and allow potent communication in the future. Basically, you will be asking them to talk to you and help you with whatever challenges you are experiencing. To quote a familiar verse, "Ask and you shall receive." The incredible gifts of the Golden Ancestors are just waiting to be opened. Your ancestors have gone through several hardships to cultivate the gems of wisdom available to you now. The resilience you are able to access has been passed down through their lineages. Additionally, have you ever wondered why you seem to pick up certain things more easily than others? Well, these are gifts from the Golden Ancestors. The more you learn to harness this magic, the faster you can access your own unimaginable gifts.

If you listen quietly, you'll realize that your Golden Ancestors have been with you this entire journey, secretly cheering you on. They are always behind the scenes, protecting you and sending you energy. When you learn to become an excellent receiver of their gifts, next-level magic begins to appear in your life. You may even hear some fun stories about your ancestors that your parents never told you as the ancestors themselves share these magical secrets with you.

Golden Ancestors Magic

Golden Ancestors Magic is a radiating golden energy that is always available to us. It carries with it every gift that has been passed down from generation to generation. From the beginning of our ancestral lineage, these mystical energies have been shared with us. Many of us have not been taught how to tap into or cultivate these gems of wisdom, and yet it is a stream of power and light that is ready to be utilized.

Every difficult moment and hardship that our ancestors went through allowed them to cultivate virtues and gifts. These gifts are passed down to each of us, and when we focus upon their energy and light, these gifts can be amplified and mastered. Emotional mastery, song and dance, food creation, all forms of athleticism, writing, artistry and artistic expression, and more are all passed down through the portals of our Golden Ancestors. Our job is to play with these energies and to make them our own.

For far too long, the focus of the world has been slightly off. We have spent too much time focusing on protecting ourselves and our assets. The simple act of tuning in to play, creativity, and the artistry of our ancestors can activate an entirely different set of genetic expression. When we begin to look for the good in our past, we will begin to see more of the good show up in the current reality. Every culture and ancestral line has energy-rich gifts such as this available—the challenge is to look for them. By focusing on our ancestral gifts, we are able to bring even more love and positivity into our lives. When we observe a hardship in our ancestral line, we can dig deeper into the gifts our ancestors received from moving through those hardships. These gems are always deep within the shadows, and instead of getting caught up observing only the surface level, when we allow ourselves to explore the depths, we can become enlightened. Herein lies the power of the Golden Ancestors, ready to shower your life with abundant gifts.

Samantha's Golden Ancestors Story

My great-grandfather was the shamanic healer of the village where he lived in Taiwan. They called them *dang gi*, which are channelers of the spirit realm. My grandmother, my *Nai Nai*, often shared stories of his miraculous healings and how the villagers loved him so dearly. She also frequently talked about his kind, loving, and compassionate heart.

One night, a married couple came to visit my great-grandfather. The husband had been coughing up blood for days, and the wife begged my great-grandfather to please see him. My great-grandfather was told the couple had five kids, and the man hadn't been able to work since he'd been sick.

My great-grandfather took one look at the husband and knew this was a dangerous mission. He said he may not be able to help them. The wife begged and pleaded. So, my great-grandfather meditated and traveled to the center of the earth. There, he saw this man's Tree of Life, and it was wilted and dried up. My great-grandfather walked over and watered the tree. Tiger Guardian came by and said that he had violated one of the karmic laws—this man was meant to die. Since my great-grandfather watered the tree, he had to take on this karma instead.

My great-grandfather returned from his journey and passed away a few days after. The other man completely healed. This was one of the bedtime stories my *Nai Nai* told me and my cousin. She also shared several other stories about my great-grandfather (her father) magically showing up in her life as she grew.

Learning about this healer wound that my great-grandfather had given me provided me so much insight into my own fears of being a healer, and it taught me how to use my superpowers appropriately. When my clairvoyant abilities opened spontaneously in 2008, after several hypnosis sessions in Taiwan, I had to process a lot of fears around my ability to see and feel other dimensions of reality. Working with my Golden Ancestors supported me in quickly processing some of these wounds since they had already cleared them in the spiritual realm. For example, I was able to have deep conversations with my great-grandfather and release some of my invisible fears with so much ease. This is one of the great benefits of working with your Golden Ancestors.

As I began to dive deeper into the world of energy medicine, I often received visits from my great-grandfather. He seemed to guide me so that I could adjust my work as needed. He had learned so much in the spiritual realm. The more I decided to connect to this energy, the more this stream of light and knowledge would simply come to me. He showed me ways I could work lighter, faster, and clearer.

I continued to create meditations within myself to connect to my ancestors. I would imagine myself bringing them fruit, flowers, water, and all of the resources they may need. I would send them beautiful, colorful clothes and vibrant materials with gold woven into the cloth. I could see their faces light up, and their energy fields charged up. They were able to send energy back to me. This is something I interacted with often. As I opened up these portals, I felt all of the immense gifts they were so excited to share with me. Cooking came easier to me, as did dancing, singing, and music in general. I allowed their love to flow into me and appreciated the gifts and insights they shared with me.

I am sure that your ancestors are also eagerly waiting for an opportunity to connect with you. See past the human versions of them and connect to the enlightened spirit of their souls. See what this awakens within you. There is so much magic available for you through this process, and through them.

Pamela's Golden Ancestors Story

Working with my Golden Ancestors was something I resisted for a long time. This was because I thought working with my ancestors meant I would be in contact with my relatives who were currently living. As I am not really close to my family, and I don't even know my father's side, the idea of working with family did not appeal to me.

However, a few years ago, when working with my spiritual life coach to move up to my next level of abundance, I discovered that a blockage I was experiencing was connected to my Golden Ancestors. The problem was that I didn't have any connection to them. I had been blocking the wisdom and gifts from my ancestors, and these very gifts could help me reach my goals with ease. After this realization, I created a beautiful altar honoring my ancestors. However, what I missed—and what a lot of my private clients also forget to do—was including ancestors from both sides of the family. I only honored my maternal ancestral side because it was the side of the family that I was most connected to and actually knew about. Since I didn't know my father's side of the family, I didn't attempted to connect to my paternal ancestors.

Then, during a healing session with another coach, I was told that one of my ancestors on my father's side had a gift for me. She said he was trying to give me the gift, but I was blocking it. That made so much sense, because I was not tapped into my father's side at all. Her message for me was that my father's side was a royal lineage—someone was a king or queen—and they had lots of magic connected to wealth that they wanted to share with me. She told me that even though I did not know my family on my father's side, it was still okay to work with those Golden Ancestors because they are still a part of my lineage.

I decided to upgrade my Golden Ancestors altar to include my father's side, honoring both sides of my family in the same space. Soon after, I had a major breakthrough in my business. The financial challenges I had been facing, which included a lack of clients, just disappeared, and this ended up being a transformational time for me. I started to be seen online and received more recognition and more clients.

In the beginning, I did feel weird connecting to the paternal side of my ancestral line, but my Golden Ancestors were very open to working with me, and there was no trauma or anything that I needed to heal in order to work with them. Therefore, even though I do not have any connection to my living relatives on my father's side, my paternal Golden Ancestors are now an important part of my practice. The energy felt really positive from the instant I connected with them. Since this experience, I have encouraged all my clients to honor their ancestors on both sides of their family, and everyone who has done so has experienced powerful shifts in their lives.

The important thing to know about your Golden Ancestors is that *you* have to make the connection. It is up to you to reach out to them and open the door to communication. Your Golden Ancestors from both sides are ready to work with you and to offer unconditional love; they have lots of wisdom, teachings, and gifts to share. Open up your heart and start asking for the magic of this connection.

I ask for opportunities and abundance from my Golden Ancestors every single day by speaking to them at my altar. If you have a different goal, or if you want to create a more intimate connection with your ancestors, try the ritual later in this chapter. It will amplify your ability to receive what you most desire, with their support.

Setting Up Your Golden Ancestors Altar

A Golden Ancestors altar is the anchor for connecting to your ancestors because it provides them a sacred space in your home. This section is going to be a little different than the other chapters because the tools that you should put on your altar will be more personalized.

Before you set up your altar, do the Meeting Your Golden Ancestors Guide meditation in the next section of the book, and make sure you ask your ancestors what they want their altar to feel like, look like, and be like. You might already have some ideas about what to put on your altar, because as soon as you decide to work with your Golden Ancestors, that connection is activated. You may have already started to receive intuitive messages and guidance from them!

Remember, your ancestors from both sides of your family have gifts for you. Don't be shy about asking for miracles and opportunities from your Golden Ancestors—they are here to support you on your earthly journey! You can choose to create two different ancestral altars or, like us, you can create one with both sides of your family represented. Here are some magical tools that are usually placed on ancestral altars:

Incense

Candles

Pictures of your ancestors[5]

Anything that belonged to your ancestors

---

5. If you do not have pictures of your ancestors, then you don't need to put any pictures on your altar. Simply write the name of the ancestor on a plaque or a piece of paper if you feel called to include them on the altar. If you do not know an ancestor's name, just write "Ancestor."

Crystals

Dirt

Salt

A bowl of water

Fruit

Sweets and desserts

These are just suggestions based on what we have learned from working with our own ancestors. It is very important that you adorn your altar with personalized tools that you feel best represent your lineage and ancestral energy.

Create a daily ceremony to honor your Golden Ancestors. It can be as simple as greeting your ancestral altar every morning, lighting a candle, saying a prayer, sharing gratitude, leaving fresh fruits and vegetables, pouring a drink for your ancestors, or lighting incense. You can also recite commands, affirmations, or mantras in front of your altar.

After you have finished setting up your Golden Ancestors altar, activate the altar by calling in your ancestral guides.

Meeting Your Golden Ancestors

Every one of us is connected to a stream of golden light that is a gift from our Golden Ancestors. Whether you are connected to your family of origin or not, this stream of light is always available to you. You don't need to know any information about your ancestors in order to connect. Rather than connecting to the personalities of your ancestors, this is a practice to connect to the Spirit aspects of your ancestors. If you were adopted, you receive a bonus, as you are able to connect to ancestors from your family of origin as well as ancestors from your adopted family, making the stream of light from your Golden Ancestors extra strong and powerful.

This meditation can be done more than once. Each time you come back to this meditation, you may receive different messages or observe frequency shifts or changes.

Get comfortable and close your eyes. As you enter the portal of connection to the Golden Ancestors, remind yourself that magical gifts await you. If you have not connected with your Golden Ancestors before, know that they have been waiting your entire lifetime to connect with you. If you have connected with them before, then this is a journey that will take you even closer to mastering the gifts and magic available for you.

Find your way to a cozy space underneath a mandarin tree. Feel the abundance of the leaves surrounding you and the bright color of the fruit lifting your spirits. You may even smell and taste the fragrant mandarin orange as you sit there in your relaxed state. You see an open grassy field all around you. There is plenty of space for your ancestors to come and be near you, and you will be able to invite in as many Golden Ancestors as you wish.

Begin to focus on your breath. Imagine sparkling golden light flowing into your lungs and throughout your body as you inhale. On the exhale, feel gold light flooding from your lungs and infusing magic into the grassy fields. Light shimmers inside of you and all around you. Golden light in, golden light out. Feel yourself raising your own light frequency in order to be in energetic harmony with your ancestors. Feel yourself sending golden light both into your past and your future.

Send streams of energy to both your maternal and paternal sides of the family. Observe the energy radiating out to them, then feel the golden energy they are sending back to you. Notice as the flow of connection between you strengthens. If you see any murky energy, watch it being washed away in the golden light. Only allow goodness to flow back into you, releasing all of the rest.

All around you, your ancestors begin to arrive. Remember that you are encountering the higher self of your ancestors, so they may not look exactly the way you remember them. You may want to imagine beautiful cushions for them to sit on, or you can invite them to sit on lotus flowers beside you. Have tea, water, fruit, and snacks ready for them. Feel the energy of celebration as you welcome your ancestors into the space with you. As you breathe the golden light in and out, you see them breathing the golden light in and out as well. You are all breathing in harmony with one another.

You may feel the ancestors organized in a sacred geometric shape or pattern in front of you or behind you, or as stated previously, you may feel them filling up the area. You may be able to clearly sense the difference between maternal and paternal energy, or the sides of your family may mingle. Decide what feels best for your energy field. Then, create a lot of golden light around you and your Golden Ancestors and lean in to the sensations of this connective golden light.

Begin to feel all of the loving energy that your ancestors have for you. They are seeing you from a higher perspective and are filled with love. Continue to breathe and move your body in a way that relaxes you and allows you to feel the flow of life. Notice how lovingly held and supported you are. Observe how much your ancestors genuinely want you to succeed. Recognize how much of this newfound energy through your connection to the Golden Ancestors will be fueling you going forward.

Take a few moments and invite either one ancestor, or a group of ancestors, to step forward. Notice how this ancestor looks. If it is a group that steps forward, notice how many are present. Then, allow yourself to receive a message from them. It may be in the form of a feeling, a color, a shape, or something else. Give them space and opportunity to connect and communicate with you.

Notice how they update the biological energy of your cells. As members of the Spirit realm, they have accessed many updates, and they are able to speed up your energetic operating system in order for spontaneous healing to occur in your physical, mental, emotional, and spiritual bodies. Give yourself time to fully receive their updated gifts and love.

Your Golden Ancestors begin to tell you stories. As you hear story after story of what they came here to share with you, notice how much more whole, grounded, and solid your body feels. It may feel as if a piece of a puzzle, missing for all these years, has finally been found. Feel your entire body buzzing with golden energy.

Ask your Golden Ancestors how often you should connect with them, and the best way for you to use this golden stream of energy to connect with one other. They may say they would like to connect once every morning or evening for five minutes, or they may say to connect only once a month. What feels good for your unique energy connection with your Golden Ancestors? Whatever agreement you come to, make sure you follow up at the designated time.

Give thanks to your Golden Ancestors. They radiate and beam so much love back to you, reminding you that they are always available and happy to provide anything you may need. They encourage you to return whenever you would like.

Gift-Receiving Golden Ancestors Ritual

No matter what you are working toward, there are gifts from your ancestors that can help you achieve your goals with ease and grace. They have already lived a life of wisdom and are ready to share their knowledge with you. Whether it's teachings about what they experienced, extra luck, or more abundance, you are supported by your Golden Ancestors.

However, your ancestors will not automatically give you gifts because they do not want to interfere with your free will. The Golden Ancestors are very respectful of your decisions—you get to make your own choices and create the life that you most desire. If you decide to ask for their help, you will discover what they have to offer you. The magic has always been there, but you have to be willing to receive it, and you have to take the initiative by asking for it.

In this ritual, you will be asking your Golden Ancestors for a specific gift that aligns with an intention you have. This is not a one-time ritual; you are welcome to return to this ritual at any time and ask for a different gift. We have noticed that our ancestral gifts need some time to integrate and manifest, so we like to fulfill the cycle of manifestation for a few of our intentions before we ask for more. To determine how many gifts you should ask for, we recommend that you reflect on how much energy and change you can handle in your life right now. For example, if you are asking for the gift of finding your soulmate *and* a new job, ask yourself, do you really have time and space for both? You do not want to overwhelm your energetic field and physical body by asking for too much, and it is never a good idea to ask for more than you think you can handle, as this will cause massive upheaval in your life. This is because there will be several changes and transitions happening at the same time as your Golden Ancestors clear the way toward what you most want.

It's very important to have fun asking for your gifts. Asking should always come from a place of joy and curiosity, not desperation. When you are asking from a place of desperation, then the energy of lack is sent out and blocks you from the magic. Instead of urgently needing what you want to manifest so that your life will be better, change your perception and choose to ask from a place of gratitude: "I love my life already, and what the ancestors bring me will add even more abundance to my life." Even if your current reality leaves much to be desired, find something you can be grateful for. This is how you can move from lacking to manifesting.

While you may be looking for evidence of change in your life after performing this ritual, it's best not to attach yourself to expectations of how things will show up for you. Miracles are miracles because they show up in ways beyond our imagination. When you ask for gifts that are the highest and best for you, trust that your Golden Ancestors will send you the very best, at the perfect time and in ways that will blow you away.

To prep for the ritual, you will first need to connect with your Golden Ancestors using the meditation in the previous section of this chapter. Afterward, gather these magical tools:

Two items, one that represents your maternal ancestors and one that represents your paternal ancestors
A small glass jar or nonflammable container with a lid
Small clear quartz crystal

Your intention (what you would like the gift to help you
    manifest)

Small piece of paper

Pen

White candle

Journal

Lighter or matches

Cleanse your sacred space and Golden Ancestors altar with
an herbal wand or spray and set up your magical tools for the
ritual. Make sure you are in a place where you won't be disturbed
for the duration of your ritual. Your ritual can be as long as you
want, depending on the time you want to stay in the energy of the
Golden Ancestors and the size of your candle.

1. On a slip of paper, write down the gift you would like to
   receive. If you do not know specifically what you want, you
   can just write, "I am open to receiving the highest and best
   gift for me at this time." When you are done writing, fold
   the paper toward you one time. Then turn it 90 degrees to
   the right and fold it toward you again. Repeat the step of
   turning and folding it one more time to the right.

2. Take your nonflammable container and put your peti-
   tion paper in it, saying your intention out loud as you do
   so, infusing it into the container. Next, drop your crystal
   inside. Then, put the lid on.

3. Next, you need to adhere your candle to the top of your
   container so that when it melts, the wax will seal the
   container shut. To stick the candle on securely, use your
   lighter or matches to melt the bottom of the candle. The

wax needs to be soft in order to adhere the candle to the lid. Then, press the bottom of the candle firmly onto the lid. Hold the candle in an upright position for a few moments so that the wax can begin to reharden.

4. When you are ready, light your candle and say your intention out loud again.

5. Please keep an eye on the candle at all times, and do not leave the flame unattended. If the candle happens to fall off the lid, re-adhere it and relight the candle, saying the same intention again. If you have to leave the room, make sure you snuff out your candle first. (Do not blow the candle out with your breath; use your fingers or a snuffer.) Later, when you are ready to complete the process, relight the candle while saying your intention. Your ritual will be finished when the candle is done burning.

6. After the candle is finished burning, you may keep this container on your altar or somewhere magical until you feel the gift has manifested or your intention is complete. Sometimes a gift is subtle, so be on the lookout for signs and experiences that validate its manifestation. Other times, we achieve our goals instantly.

7. When your intentions have manifested, you can then open the container. Cleanse the crystal and the container with Florida water or smoke from an herbal wand. Feel free to keep the paper with your intent, or bury it in your yard. You could also throw it away since its work is complete, which is what we typically do.

Sacred Code Activations

The Golden Ancestors can be a phenomenal resource for you. It is great to call upon them in moments when you have forgotten who you are or are doubting your powers or abilities. The Golden Ancestors can quickly reboot your system and remind you of your gifts. When you want to discover even more of your own unique skills, the Golden Ancestors can add insight and support. Using the Golden Ancestors Commandment is a fast way to reconnect with them and to receive their rich love and wisdom.

Golden Ancestors Commandment

"Dear Golden Ancestors, as a direct expression of the Divine, I ask for mystical support from all realms to nourish every aspect of me. I ask to be powered up with joy and celebration from other realms. Golden Ancestors, I give you permission to update my biological body, and the trillions of cells within me, to a higher energy so that I can fully align with my soul. I ask permission to quickly and efficiently move through lessons in my families' ancestral timelines and to open up portals to magical manifestations beyond what I can comprehend with my own imagination. Golden Ancestors, I give you permission to awaken the gift of sight within me so that I can collapse time and create from an even more blissful state. I ask that any and all unhelpful tendencies in our family ancestral line be washed and cleared away by your golden light. I am open to seeing the world and my life from a new perspective, accelerating my capacity and ability to create with joy and ease. Thank you for these miraculous gifts. I seal this transmission with love and light, and I see this benefitting all those close to me and all those around me."

Golden Ancestors Mantras

Golden Ancestor mantras are a tremendous energy upgrade. Think of a hose that has a kink in it: once adjusted, all of a sudden large amounts of water flood through. You may feel similarly while working with this level of light energy and love. As you work through these mantras, be open and ready to receive, and be extra observant about what begins to show up in your everyday life.

You may decide to slightly adjust the wording of one or all of these mantras to make them even more powerful for you. Trust your intuition.

- Each and every day, I am lovingly supported and fueled by the light of my Golden Ancestors.
- Powerful gifts that benefit me are passed down by my Golden Ancestors. These may include gifts of art, music, dance, cuisine, organization, and more.
- I am powerfully protected by my Golden Ancestors in every way and in every dimension.
- I am deeply and immensely loved by my Golden Ancestors.
- All of the good I do each day is lovingly sent back to my Golden Ancestors.
- I open and unlock sacred desires and magic abilities from my Golden Ancestors.
- My Golden Ancestors turn keys and open doors that lead immense love, abundance, and life to flow into my body.

- My kidneys are continuously updating to allow more of my Golden Ancestors' power and light to flow through my body and supercharge me.[6]
- I am always powerfully guided toward the quickest route to achieving what I want, and it is the most joyful path provided by my Golden Ancestors.

Golden Ancestors Ascension Prompts

Create a sacred space and get ready to tune in. You're about to activate a very powerful stream of energy between you and your Golden Ancestors. There is so much love available for you here.

Take some time to think and feel between each question listed. You may find yourself skipping around as you read. That's perfectly okay—find what you're most drawn to and start there. Trust your intuition to guide you as you awaken new streams of energy within yourself.

1. If there was one ancestral trait that you could embody, what would it be and why? How would it feel to really own this trait?
2. What do you admire about your ancestral lineage?
3. What emotions come up for you when you feel the love of your Golden Ancestors? If you knew that they were powerfully supporting you every day, how would you feel?
4. Now that you know you have access to your ancestors' power and wisdom, how will you choose to move through life even more confidently and powerfully?

---

6. Note: In Chinese Medicine, the kidneys and kidney meridian store your ancestral life force energy. By updating the kidneys, you allow yourself to receive more golden light from your ancestors.

5. If you could pick one family theme to heal today, what would that be? What would it feel like to have this healed? What would change for you and others?

6. Write a letter to your Golden Ancestors. What is something that's been on your heart that you've been wanting to share with them? How do you feel after writing this letter?

Channeled Message from the Golden Ancestors

"Your family constellation is a sacred geometrical shape and an energy imprint in the stars. See the beauty that is available for you here, and you will unlock a world of marvelous wonder that you never imagined was available to you. Soften the mind. Look past the hardships. See the gifts. Trust that they have all been here, waiting for you this entire time."

—Golden Ancestors

Chapter Seven
Kuan Yin

A crisis is an opportunity riding the dangerous wind.
—Chinese Proverb

With one thousand hands and one thousand eyes on each palm, Kuan Yin can see every being in the world. She offers support, guidance, and light to those that call upon her. This is why she is known as the bodhisattva of compassion.

Traditionally, in Buddhist philosophy, once a being has reached enlightenment, they become a buddha. So, what is a bodhisattva? This is an incredibly compassionate being on the path to enlightenment and Buddhahood. Bodhisattvas have seemingly unending love, compassion, and energy.

While we may refer to Kuan Yin as a goddess in this context, in the Buddhist philosophy, buddhas and bodhisattvas have evolved into a being that has no gender. Kuan Yin is depicted as a goddess to represent softness, gentleness, and compassion, and yet the truth of her being is genderless. This is a reminder that we all have powerful feminine and masculine energies within us, and that each of us is completely whole within ourself.

Kuan Yin is very respected in Asian cultures and is frequently prayed to. Throughout the Far East, she may be known by different names, such as *Gwan-eum* in Korea, *Kuan Eim* in Thailand, *Kanzeon* in Japan, and *Quan Am* in Vietnam. In Taiwan and in the Buddhist temples we have visited, she is known as *Guanshiyin Pusah*, which, when we translate it from Chinese to English, means "observing the sounds (or cries) of the world." Not only is she a very respected and popular goddess in the East, but her popularity has expanded to the West as well.

The goddess Kuan Yin can be seen in many forms. Usually, she is portrayed sitting on a lotus or standing. She wears a white robe, symbolizing purity, and has a halo of light surrounding her head as well as necklaces fit for royalty in the Chinese tradition. You may see her depicted as the goddess with a thousand hands. Our favorite representation of Kuan Yin is when she is holding a water vase in her right hand and a willow branch in her left hand. The vase contains the nectar of life and is a symbol of good fortune; it is said to heal any disease or dark, illusionary thoughts. The willow is used to sprinkle the nectar's blessings. Another version of Kuan Yin rides a dragon, and many fishermen prayed to her as the goddess of the Southern Sea. Regardless of how she presents herself, know that if you chant her name or her mantra, "Om mani padme hum" (pronounced om money pad-may home), she will come to you and bring incredible miracles. Even though this mantra is in Sanskrit, it is used all over the world.

With Kuan Yin (and with many of the spiritual beings we share about in this book), the key is to reach out and ask for help. Asking for divine assistance reflects that you are in charge and are claiming what you want to create in life. Know that you are always going to be fully in control of your own decisions, even with spiritual intervention, and that you are ultimately the one who must take action. Also keep in mind that spiritual beings support manifestation from a place of unconditional love. When you ask Kuan Yin for assistance, this bodhisattva must always confirm that you are asking for the highest good for yourself and all affected. Then, she will step in and offer guidance.

When you ask Spirit for help, you are not surrendering or sacrificing anything to them. Kuan Yin, like other beings, honors your power and knows you are also a god(dess) currently in physical form. You are a direct expression of the cosmos, and she supports you and reminds you of your own creative powers.

Kuan Yin Magic

Kuan Yin's magic is so freely gifted to us every day, we may accidentally take this magic for granted. It is the love of the Cosmic Mother. She gifts us everything that is for our highest growth and evolution, everything that we need and more. Her reflection can be seen in the abundant rainforests that provide a variety of foods, medicines, adventures, animals, and life itself in the air we breathe. Her compassion is beyond human understanding, because even if we violate every law and cross every boundary, when we ask for her love, she gives it to us, lovingly and freely. If we accidentally neglect or damage the gifts she's given us, she easily forgives and goes back to giving yet again. This does not give us permission to simply, and without cause, make mistake after mistake. However, it reminds us that all aspects of ourselves are loved and lovable, and we are constantly evolving and growing. Also, we are given infinite opportunities to learn and grow, and Kuan Yin is an incredible example of this.

Kuan Yin's vision is so far beyond our own. She can see past the illusions of current discomfort or perceived mistakes. She sees the eternal magical being that we are, as extensions of Source energy, having a physical experience. Her focus and gaze will always be upon the most positive aspects of who we are because that is all she sees and knows. Her love gives us space to course-correct and return to our sacred path. Simply calling her name and being in her energy field will fill you with the deepest love of the Cosmic Mother.

The power and love of Kuan Yin as Cosmic Mother is a power beyond what we can comprehend. This is not the same energy of worry, concern, or protection we may at times experience from a human mother. Cosmic Mother will ferociously allow you to make your own mistakes, if they are for your highest good, while still holding space and guiding you every step of the way so that you always land safely. In dramatic, violent situations, she will quickly bring about light and truth. When you are in any kind of danger, call her name, and she will immediately arrive; miracles will happen faster than your human mind can comprehend. Cosmic Mother will nourish you in ways you may not even have known were missing.

This is the magic of Kuan Yin. Call upon her often and form a deep connection with her magic. She is always available for you.

Samantha's Kuan Yin Story

When I was still in my mother's womb, she saw a statue of Kuan Yin as she walked by a beautiful lake in Taiwan. She looked at the lotus flower beneath Kuan Yin's feet and decided my Chinese name would be Ding Bao Lien (Ding/Ting for my Chinese last name, and Bao Lien for Lotus Flower), and so my name became Samantha Ting Lotus Blossom Brown.

Kuan Yin has been close to me for as long as I can remember. My grandma would often take me to the temple to bring incense to Kuan Yin, and I have felt very protected by her so many times in my life. When I went to the temple as a young child, headmasters would always say I had a lot of *Yuan*, or destiny, with Kuan Yin, and that I should make sure to take time to connect with her, so I did.

One of my favorite stories involving Kuan Yin occurred when I was in my early twenties. For most of my life up until that point, I had received straight A's, but when I moved to Shanghai, I began receiving B's and B-pluses on a consistent basis instead. It may seem silly to feel so stressed out over receiving B's for the first time in your life, but that was my reality. It felt like it didn't matter how hard I studied; I didn't know how to get ahead. I felt so frustrated that studying more wasn't changing the situation. My health started going downhill. I was having trouble sleeping since I was so worried about my grades. Eventually, I started to develop panic attacks and became unable to sleep the entire week of my exams. All the exams were in Chinese, and I had just learned how to read and write Chinese the summer before. While I had always been able to speak Mandarin Chinese, reading and writing it was completely new for me.

My mother was always great at finding solutions, so one summer, when I was in Taipei, Taiwan, she looked for a hypnotherapist for me. She told me that she didn't feel like my current level of anxiety was good for me, and we really needed to be proactive about it. She found the perfect hypnotherapist, and during our first session together, we resolved one of my deepest abandonment wounds. Ever since I was a small child, I had this very intense feeling of abandonment when my parents were away. During my first hypnosis session, I traveled to a past life in which it was revealed I had been an infant in a basket, left on the front doorstep of a family in Korea. The father adored me, but the mother felt threatened by me. She had three other children and always gave me extra chores. One day, she poured hot water on my leg, and it created this mark—a birthmark I have on my right thigh, even now. To heal the wound, I was taken to the village's shamanic healer. This is when I vowed to learn and practice Chinese Medicine.

The strangest things began to happen after my first few hypnosis sessions. First, I began to see angels and guides. Second, I remember crossing the street one day and thinking, *There are no thoughts in my head.* My mind felt completely empty. I was used to having lots of worried thoughts, yet at that point, my mind was totally clear. This incredible sense of calm and ease had washed over me. That same night, I went to the temple with my mom to celebrate Kuan Yin's birthday. As part of the ritual, everyone wore black, and many people were crying as they read the sutra and repented for their past wrongdoings. Since my third eye had been opened, I was able to see what was really happening. Above the temple, I saw all of the buddhas and bodhisattvas dancing and wearing colorful clothes. I saw ribbons of all colors, woven with gold. They were dancing, singing, and eating the most delicious foods. This was a moment of realization for me—I realized that somehow I had been trained to focus on and observe the suffering of the world, when in truth, life was actually filled with so much beauty and wonder. I saw in that moment that life was meant to be a celebration filled with colors! It became so clear to me.

It was also then that I saw a huge image of Kuan Yin pouring a drop of water from her vase, a drop of water that encompassed the entire temple. She was activating the joyful consciousness of all of us in that moment. After that, I was never again able to sit and do eight hours of mantras in an uncomfortable position, wearing clothes that I didn't really feel were a reflection of me. I knew that freedom and life and celebration were the real path.

Kuan Yin has continued to show up in my life, and I am always grateful for it. I highly encourage you to connect with her and chant her mantra to see what magical and delightful gifts she may bring your way.

Pamela's Kuan Yin Story

My connection to Kuan Yin is not just one story, but a combination of many experiences that led me to realize the multitude of gifts she offers. As Samantha and I were writing this book, I experienced additional revelations about her.

I had been initiated with Kuan Yin when I was little, praying to her and claiming her as my goddess in the temples. When I was four, a master at the temple told me that she was my personal goddess, and she was who I should mainly pray to. So, I was given mala beads for this purpose, and I have been praying to her ever since. The funny thing is, I never connected her Chinese name to the English version, "Kuan Yin," until recently, while talking to Sam about this book. Since I moved to America at a young age, I associated Chinese words to an object or item, not their translation, so I thought Kuan Yin's Chinese name was one deity and her English name was another. I was even worried that I wouldn't be able to contribute to this chapter because I thought I never had a connection with Kuan Yin—until I realized she is the same goddess I've been praying to for decades! The Universe works in mysterious ways. Now that I realize our connection, I want to share all the ways I have connected with Kuan Yin throughout my life.

One thing Kuan Yin had an impact on was my perfectionism. For years, I thought that I needed to be perfect. With Kuan Yin's assistance, I realized I didn't have to force things to happen, and instead I could trust in divine timing for my highest good. Another negative programming I had claimed during the early stages of my life's journey was that I had to accomplish a lot early on in life or I couldn't be successful. Therefore, by the time I was in my twenties, whenever an opportunity came up, I would give the excuse that I was "too old." This limiting belief came up for me every time I wanted to expand and evolve. For example, I didn't graduate from college because, at the time, I didn't have the money to finish, and when I was making enough money to finally go at the age of twenty-two, I told myself I was too old to go back to school. There was also a time that I wanted to become an air traffic controller, and I made up the excuse that I was too old, even though I was still young enough to be accepted into the program at that time.

It was during my thirties that I snapped out of the cycle of thinking I was not enough and too old to do anything. As part of my spiritual work with Kuan Yin, I was able to release a lot of old beliefs and patterns that no longer served me, freeing me to chase all of my dreams no matter what age I may be! I am where I am today because I tapped into the compassionate energies of this goddess for myself, adopted the programming of already living a fulfilled life, and stopped trying to reach or grasp external "things" like more money, a better job, or material objects. The more I connected with Kuan Yin, I learned to be happy where I am now, in the present moment, and the need to compare myself to others disappeared. I learned that comparing where I was in my life to others' distracted me from focusing on my own journey and my own joy.

From this new perspective, I now know that I am never too old—or too young—to accomplish anything, because things are always aligned with my best and highest good and the perfection of divine timing. There is never an opportunity or dream that is too big for any of us. If we desire it, then it—or something better—is in our destiny. All our wants are what lead us to know ourselves and to our life purpose, even if they seem out of reach at the time. Kuan Yin always reminds me that if there is anything that I want, I just have to set my intention and follow the path to manifesting it. I might be more successful than my wildest dreams, or something better suited for me may appear, but either way, everything is part of my unique life experience, and the journey itself is what brings me joy.

We encourage you to make your life an adventure. Go out and find the person or thing that can help you reach your goals. You are magic, and you are the co-creator of your life. You can manifest anything you desire. If you need a little help, reach out and ask Kuan Yin for guidance, as she is always there for you. All you need to do is invoke her name and request her assistance, and she will come to your aid.

When I was young, I listened to a Kuan Yin mantra song every single night and felt protected. If I felt lonely, I reached out to the goddess and could sense that someone was watching over me. I always knew she was real, not only because of all of the results I saw in my life after working with her, but also because one of my family friends took a photo of the clouds on a plane ride, and when they printed the photo, it was a black-and-white image of Kuan Yin. She has been by my side, helping me, through so much of my life, and she does the same for so many others I know and have worked with. I hope you can connect with her too, and experience your own miracles.

Setting Up Your Kuan Yin Altar

Praying to Kuan Yin can help you accomplish things in all areas of life. This bodhisattva is here to gently guide you toward the realization of your intentions, and she does so with loving grace. She is a compassionate, all-knowing deity who will provide insight, and she will do so lovingly. Set up your Kuan Yin altar to hold space for honoring and connecting to this divine bodhisattva, to call in your desires, and to be fully present in the moment.

Here are some tools related to Kuan Yin's energy that you can use to decorate your altar. These suggestions were guided by Kuan Yin in a meditative channeling that we performed for this book. Feel free to add tools that are familiar to you or any others we have discussed. Always remember the energy of Kuan Yin is full of compassion, unconditional love, and kindness.

Kuan Yin Crystals

Aquamarine
Jade
Aventurine

Kuan Yin Colors

White
Blue
Pastels

Kuan Yin Symbols

Lotus flower
Sandalwood
Water

Kuan Yin Food Offerings

Sweet cakes
Rice
Fruits
Vegetables

Kuan Yin Tarot Cards

The Lovers
Judgement
The High Priestess

You can create a daily ceremony to honor Kuan Yin. It can be as simple as greeting your Kuan Yin altar every morning by lighting a candle, saying your prayers, giving thanks, offering food and drink, lighting incense, or stating an intention for the day. You could also recite commands, affirmations, or mantras in front of your altar.

After you have finished setting up your Kuan Yin altar, activate the altar by calling in the bodhisattva using the instructions in the next section.

Meeting Your Kuan Yin Guide

Kuan Yin is the bodhisattva of divine blessings and compassion, and with the sweetest touch. When you desire nourishment, love, and intimacy at the deepest level, call upon Kuan Yin. Her compassionate spirit is ready and available for you, especially when you are experiencing heavy or dark moments. Simply activate your awareness of her and she will arrive, showing up for you in the most miraculous of ways.

In Benebell Wen's book *The Tao of Craft*, she explains how using mantras and reciting the name of Kuan Yin are similar to radio frequencies.[7] Oftentimes, when you find yourself in chaos, a bad mood, or a difficult situation, it is simply because your body and brain are tuned into a specific frequency that may feel frazzled. To quickly reboot your energy fields and to access a new frequency, connect with the bodhisattva Kuan Yin.

Remember that Kuan Yin is an eternal being, and she is infinite energy. From her perspective, she is very happy when we take the time to tune in and connect with her. This never depletes her energy and, in fact, generates more good energy, because energy is infinite.

Take a moment to create a sacred space. Perhaps you are sitting on your favorite meditation cushion. You may want to have a vase of flowers in front of you. Having mala beads in hand is also a beautiful gesture.

Once you are comfortable, invite gold light to fill the room around you. Close your eyes and find yourself sitting underneath the mandarin tree. Smell the fragrance of the oranges and the uplifting sensations that this scent brings you. Feel a light smile come onto your face, a smile that arrives from the inside out.

---

7. Wen, *The Tao of Craft*, 147.

Use the mantra "Om mani padme hum," repeating it 108 times. There are usually 108 beads on most traditional mala beads. As you speak, feel the heads of the mala beads. When you've reached the bead you touched when you began, you'll know that you've chanted the mantra 108 times. While you chant, envision pink ribbons of light flowing in and out of your heart space. Be in the resonance of unconditional love as you call upon Kuan Yin with speed and ease. Notice all other energies shake off your body as your energy field begins to fill with pink light. Notice your energy vibrating at a higher frequency, letting you know you have moved toward closer resonance with Kuan Yin.

As your frequency becomes higher and higher, notice as Kuan Yin enters the space and sits beside you. You can feel the radiant love that emanates from her. Just being near Kuan Yin's energy increases your vibration, and she assists you in raising your energetic field to a higher vibrational consciousness that aligns with your current timeline. Everything in your mind and body softens. You feel a sense of ease in her presence, and you know that wonderful things are about to be revealed to you. As you sit with Kuan Yin, shortcuts to life's challenges begin to be revealed to you, shortcuts that you never thought possible. You begin to see that every answer and solution has been with you the entire time, and that they are more simple than you might have expected.

Kuan Yin places her hand over your crown chakra and brings golden light into your essence. Your entire body shimmers with delight. The deepest and most profound sense of love washes over you. Feeling this sensation of love opens up a whole new world for you. You begin to see the cosmos and the multiverse within your own body. Your cells light up with colors, bright lights, and streams of consciousness. As you witness the trillions of cells that you are made of, you become aware of a deep, reverent self-love.

Self-love leads to activation and awakening. Your breath deepens as you continue to connect with Kuan Yin.

As this compassionate energy continues to flow inside you, you experience a deeper and more profound love than you have ever experienced. "This is your power," Kuan Yin whispers to you and gently smiles. The initiation is now complete. She leaves the space after letting you know you can connect with her at any time. Each time you connect with her, a new message and a new initiation will be waiting for you. This meditation was just the beginning of many transmissions.

Begin to return to your surroundings by wiggling your fingers and toes. You may feel the lightness and brightness of your newly upgraded energy field. A sense of peace washes over you as your newfound serenity is birthed. As you go about your day, you may view the world through new eyes and a new perspective, one of greater ease.

Seeking Kuan Yin Ritual

Kuan Yin is a compassionate and powerful bodhisattva that can illuminate answers or clues to help you solve your challenges. There are always challenges in life, even for people who have been on a spiritual path for a long time, as they are how we grow and expand. The difference between an enlightened practitioner and someone who has just started on the path is how challenges are perceived. Think of each problem as an opportunity for you to evolve instead of something that is keeping you stuck. Try to see it as an invitation to find a solution and to move forward.

This beautiful ritual will allow you to receive divine guidance and find the answers you seek with greater ease and in a more timely manner. By invoking the bodhisattva Kuan Yin in this way, you will be able to create your own synchronicities in life, aligning you more readily and fully to your desires. You will be using Kuan Yin's mantra "Om mani padme hum" to call on her.

The most important part of this ritual is patience. You may have to patiently wait to receive messages, and even then, you must patiently allow your journey to unfold. With Kuan Yin's assistance, you will be learning to cultivate your inner power and to co-create a reality that is aligned with your purpose and awards you with blessings and fulfillment.

To prep for the ritual, you will first need to connect with your Kuan Yin guide using the meditation in the previous section of this chapter. Afterward, gather these magical tools:

Drawing or printed picture of Kuan Yin, or a statue of her
Your intention (what blessing you would like to receive from Kuan Yin)
Journal
Pen
White candle
Mala beads (optional)

Cleanse your sacred space and Kuan Yin altar with an herbal wand or spray and set up your magical tools for the ritual. Make sure you are in a place where you won't be disturbed for the duration of your ritual. Your ritual can be as long as you want, depending on the time you want to stay in the energy of the Kuan Yin and the size of your candle.

1. While in front of your magical tools and your altar, take deep breaths and bring your awareness to the present

moment. Light your white candle as you say your hopes for this ritual out loud.

2. After lighting your candle, sit in lotus pose on the floor and close your eyes. Begin to chant the mantra "Om mani padme hum." Chant this powerful mantra 108 times to invoke Kuan Yin, all the while focusing on your intention.[8] You may use mala beads at this time, if you wish, to assist you as you chant. If you don't have mala beads, you can also count the incantations of the mantra with your fingers or in your mind. Don't stress too much on counting—your main focus should be immersing yourself in the sound and feel of the mantra.

3. When you are done with your chant, open your eyes and look at your Kuan Yin statue or image. Verbalize your intention one more time, giving thanks to the goddess for bringing you this wish. Make sure to state your intention as if it has already happened.

4. As your candle is burning, take out your journal and start listing twenty-two ways to achieve your goals, even if the idea seems too challenging at this moment. Write down whatever comes to mind first, as these are downloads you are receiving from Kuan Yin. Whether you take action on all of them or not, each idea will create new inspiration,

---

8. Chanting a mantra 108 times originated in Hinduism, but with the movement of Buddhism, it was adopted in China by the seventh century and is used by many masters, monks, and practitioners. You can also say the mantra three, eleven, or thirteen times if 108 is too much. These are believed to be powerful auspicious numbers and have been taught to us by sound alchemy and Kundalini yoga instructors (Cushman, *A Little Bit of Mantras*, chap. 4). Choose the number that feels right for you.

taking you one step closer to your goals. If twenty-two ideas were easy to write, then write thirty-three. The goal is to get to a point where you feel like you don't have any more ideas, and then writing five to ten more after that point. Doing so will allow you to expand your success container and to receive more abundance.

5. When you are finished writing all the ways you could take action to accomplish your goals, circle the three that you feel most drawn to right now. They might be the ideas that bring you the most joy, or they might just stand out to you for some reason. If you are being called to more than three, then circle them too. Let your intuition guide you.

6. Once you have circled the actions you're most drawn to, set your journal aside and let the candle burn out. Do not leave your candle unattended after it is lit. It is always best if the candle can burn in its entirety. However, if you have to leave the room before the candle has fully melted, you may snuff it out. Then, when you are ready to finish the ritual, you can relight the candle and say your intention again. The ritual is only fully activated once the candle has stopped burning. When the candle has finished burning, you can dispose of leftover wax in the trash can.

7. The most important thing of all is to take action! Go out and do the three (or more) things you circled on your list. If you dedicate yourself to this magic and show Kuan Yin how serious you are about fulfilling your wish, you will be rewarded! For the next three days, be aware of messages from songs, books, people, or even random things suddenly appearing in your path. A powerful sign to look out

for are divine numbers like 111, 222, 333, and so on. These
are telling you that you are on the right track!

8. Make sure to visit your altar daily to share with Kuan Yin
what you have accomplished, what you are doing next,
and how you feel. Be mindful about what you are claiming
when speaking to her—if you claim it is easy, then it will
be easy, but if you keep saying "This is so hard," then it will
be hard. Any time you need a boost of energy or guidance,
chant the mantra "Om mani padme hum" and ask for
Kuan Yin's help.

Sacred Code Activations

The rich compassion of Kuan Yin is far beyond what our human
minds can comprehend. As a species, some say that humans are
still in their infancy when it comes to the actual experience of
love. The perfect time to connect with Kuan Yin is when you'd
like to increase self-love and compassion. Kuan Yin helps you
soften the edges and see the world for the perfection that it
already is. She will open your eyes to the beauty, ease, and love
that is already available for you in the here and now. This commandment is perfect to come back to when you need to get your
brain and body back into a solution-oriented state of being. Kuan
Yin will always lovingly guide you back to the magic of the present moment.

Kuan Yin Commandment

"Compassionate bodhisattva Kuan Yin, as a direct expression of
the Divine, I ask that you infuse more life, love, and celebration
into my world. Allow me to feel ease where I see hardness. Teach

me to soften my thoughts and bring peace to my heart. Guide me in seeing and trusting the flow of life. In areas where I am controlling, teach me to trust. Open my body, mind, and spirit to the multidimensional realms of receiving that I may not currently be able to see in my three-dimensional body. Increase my capacity to be an excellent receiver of light, love, and bliss. Open up doors, portals, and pathways so that I may fall into the love of the Creator. Raise my vibration so that I can see the world with new eyes and choose the joyful path that is available for me and for everyone. May this prayer be sealed with gold light and love."

Kuan Yin Mantras

While working with Kuan Yin's mantras, you must also focus more on the celebration of life. Notice the miniscule moments that can bring joy. When you're happy about the little things, you're sending a signal to yourself and to the Universe that you would like to receive more of them.

Mantras are nourishing. Know that when you're reciting words that make you feel good, then those words are the right nutrients for you in the moment. Feed yourself beautiful words and thoughts to create even more beautiful experiences in your life. Kuan Yin is with you in all of your creations.

Use Kuan Yin mantras to keep yourself in a high-vibrational state. You may decide to focus on one or more listed here, or you may want to create your own. Recording and listening to a mantra may be helpful; you could also write it down or recite it to a friend. Listen to your intuition.

- Every day of my life deserves celebration, and I am open to receiving every drop of goodness the day has for me.

- As a multidimensional being, I am capable of receiving more than I have already experienced.

- Knowing that I have evolved, I give myself permission to experience and to enjoy the sweet things in life.

- Each day, I allow myself to receive more and to celebrate more.

- I know that the better it gets, the better it gets—and I am ready for it to be even better than I can imagine.

- I know and trust that the Universe delivers everything that is meant for me.

- In each and every moment, I am completely safe and protected by the powers of the Universe.

Kuan Yin Ascension Prompts

Beauty is a superpower. Pleasure is a superpower. Asking yourself the right questions is another kind of superpower. Kuan Yin has a kind of soft, powerful magic. She reminds you that slowing down is how you speed up in life. The quality that you infuse into an experience is where the magic is. Come to these ascension prompts when you want to see the world through the lens of Kuan Yin. Let her remind you of the beauty that is already here. Feeling good will actually change the results you receive and the things you experience in life. Sometimes it is the tiniest shift that creates the most profound transformation.

1. Where in your world can you create more moments of celebration? How can you create future moments to celebrate, and how can you schedule in the celebration before the thing you desire has even happened?

2. In what ways can you make your current world more beautiful? Could you make your food more colorful? Could you place flowers on your desk? What small adjustments would make your world feel more calm, peaceful, and serene?

3. What words can you use to shower love on the people around you? Are there little compliments that you can share here and there? Who in your life would benefit most from this?

4. In what ways can you slow down? Can you savor each sip of tea? Can you take a moment to feel the sunshine and admire the sky? What tiny moments of bliss can you create for yourself throughout the day?

5. If you knew that love, beauty, and joy mattered in your life, what would you do differently? What new decisions would you make?

Channeled Message from Kuan Yin

"The world is more colorful, beautiful, and brilliant than it seems. Focus on seeing more of the celebration of life in order to create more to celebrate. Take your attention away from what you cannot control. Rather, trust in the flow of life, as all is created in accordance with divine timing."

—KUAN YIN

Chapter Eight
The Laughing Buddha

❋

A smile will gain you ten more years of life.
—Chinese Proverb

A fair warning from the Laughing Buddha: as you step into the energies of this chapter, you may find yourself overwhelmed with joy at random times. When this happens, it is confirmation that you are on the right track and should continue to pursue your work with the Laughing Buddha. If you want to activate the miracles of celebration and success right now, go ahead and put a smile on your face. That's right—smile and feel your energy lift and your heart open. You are in for a treat with this chapter. Cheers!

The Laughing Buddha says, "It's not about living a perfect life, but a life that is perfect for each of us." Everyone is unique and has different desires. We all have own our wants and needs, and we don't have to be afraid to claim them. Regardless of what society, friends, or family may say, there isn't anything that we have to do or be in order to be successful—we determine our own success. The Laughing Buddha sets the example of living life on our own terms. What brings Laughing Buddha the most joy is sitting around, relaxing, laughing, and having a good time.

A statue of the Laughing Buddha usually represents him relaxing and smiling. He is portrayed with a bald head and a protruding belly. The belly represents the powerful qi energy he has cultivated for prosperity, luck, and joy. Sometimes he will also be carrying a bag in his hand, which symbolizes a person's struggles and frustrations—he is willing to hold this bag on behalf of all who need assistance. Many statues also show the Laughing Buddha sitting on money or gold. He is a very popular and auspicious symbol in feng shui, utilized to bring in good fortune. It is best to place a Laughing Buddha statue facing the front door, near the entrance of the home, to show the world that you are welcoming more abundance and wealth into your life. A popular magical practice taught to us as little girls was to rub Laughing Buddha's belly for good luck whenever we passed by him. We were also taught the importance of asking for what we wanted as we were rubbing his belly and then thanking him when we were done.

The Laughing Buddha has different origins throughout Asia. According to stories from monks in Taiwanese temples that we heard when we were growing up, Laughing Buddha was a monk named Budai who was always happy and filled with joy. In the stories our parents told us, he is said to be the future Buddha. Like Shakyamuni Buddha was the main Buddha of our era, Laughing Buddha (also called Maitreya Buddha) will have the same teacher role that Shakyamuni Buddha had, and he will teach generations to come. In Japan, *Budai*, which means cloth sack, is called *Hotei*. The Laughing Buddha is one of the Japanese Shinto Gods of Luck. No matter where he is or who he represents, he brings good luck to anyone who is ready to call upon the abundance that he has to offer.

Laughing Buddha Magic

Laughing Buddha magic is one of the most profound remedies that we have access to in our time. When we slow down to look at a situation, we can always find a place that holds laughter or new life if we look hard enough, even when it feels difficult. We live in a world that is simply a play, with characters and scenes and stages. When we take a step back and look at life in this way, we may be able to see how hilarious the entire experience of it all is.

You may find yourself frustrated by a situation, but if you take a minute to zoom out, you'll realize that you are simply a tiny spec in an infinite Universe. Within that infinite Universe, there is never-ending time. The very moments that we consider difficult simply fade away as we realize how everything adds color, flavor, and at times, entertainment to this thing we call life. In difficult moments, we may find it hard to laugh, but when we look back years down the road, we oftentimes find the joy in those experiences as well. As we step into greater emotional mastery, Laughing Buddha is with us to demonstrate how quickly we can decide to return to and access our joy. Joy is always available to us, no matter what, at any time and in any situation. Making the choice to find the humor in a situation can bring such a fresh perspective to all areas of life. We may find that when we are laughing, those around us cannot help but laugh too.

Laughing Buddha magic is the pure, powerful pleasure spark of the Universe. So much is available for you when you tune in to this frequency. When a task feels hard or difficult, you can tune in to the ability to make yourself laugh and to find the joy within that task. This simple shift in perspective may relax you so much, you find the difficult task to be joyful and filled with light. Masters that fully understand the magic of the Laughing Buddha know how to quickly access this state. As you continue your practice, you will find that this state becomes second nature.

The world begins to heal itself as more and more people access this realm of joy and play. We have immense gratitude for Laughing Buddha magic.

Samantha's Laughing Buddha Story

Have you heard the phrase "The better it gets, the better it gets"? When I connect with the Laughing Buddha, this is what I am reminded of. When I supercharge a moment and decide to feel really, really good in the present, I am paving a path that will attract more good things to me in the future.

The Laughing Buddha has always been a close friend of mine. Growing up in Taiwan, my dad and I would walk a paved path in the mountains to find the large, golden Laughing Buddha that was along it. This was our routine every morning. The sun would beam on our faces as we walked through the tropical leaves and trees, up the windy path, until we found ourselves standing in front of the Laughing Buddha. I always found my dad laughing too. In a way, he was an embodiment of the Laughing Buddha, and he always reminded me that things were never as hard or as serious as they seemed.

One sparkling morning, I woke up and heard the words *Santa Barbara*. This ended up being a profound moment for me: first of all, because I had never heard of the city before, and also because my intuition usually didn't come in the form of clairaudience. I started googling the city and thought it was so beautiful that I created a vision board with lots of photos of Santa Barbara on it.

I had been noticing that the dreary weather in Vancouver, Washington, wasn't really resonating with me, but I didn't really know what I wanted. However, I had been asking for more joy in my life, and the Laughing Buddha heard my prayers. A year after that fateful morning, I decided to visit the city for a week, and I fell in love with it. Another year after that, I moved to Santa Barbara, California. I didn't know or realize that a city so magical, fun, and beautiful existed! I loved all the people, the architecture, and the plants in Santa Barbara—the whole city felt so classy and vibrant.

Moving to a new state was a bold and brave leap for me, and the Laughing Buddha guided me every step of the way. Once I moved to Santa Barbara, so many wonderful things began to happen. My logical side had been worried about meeting new people and building up my business again, but each step was just laid out in front of me! One day, the Laughing Buddha guided me to have brunch at a specific place, and I met this fabulous woman. She invited me to a party and introduced me to twenty other magical women. From there, my friend circle grew, and with all of the sunshine in my life, I had ended up having so much more fun working on my business that my online coaching really took off.

At times, my mind would get really serious, and the Laughing Buddha would keep reminding me that things were always more joyful than they seemed, and that I needed to simply relax and enjoy the ride.

In those moments when you have absolutely no idea what you're going to do next, relax, play, remain open to possibilities, surrender, and tune in to the Laughing Buddha. You'll begin to see that everything in the world has the potential for joy, and you will begin to create miracles.

Pamela's Laughing Buddha Story

The Laughing Buddha has been in my life since I was young. I remember going to the temple and rubbing the Buddha's big belly for good luck in Taiwan. I always tried to do things that brought me joy, surround myself with laughter, and be open to good fortune. However, I was still unsure if I was making the right decisions sometimes. In those moments, I would talk to Laughing Buddha. This is a story about one of those times.

I was invited to join a weekend entrepreneurial event. I wasn't too sure what to expect at the event because I did not know a lot of the people from the community, but a couple of my best business buds were attending, so I decided to go too. I did a Laughing Buddha ritual before the event because I wanted to have a really good time and have every day feel like a celebration. I also wanted to network and secure some collaborations, and maybe meet a new client or two. As I was attuning my consciousness and awareness to the Laughing Buddha, I received a very specific message from him to go to an area with a lot of flowers. I wrote the message down and kept in mind that I should go and look for such a space at the event. When the ritual was completed, I felt super validated in my decision to go to the event and knew that it was going to be amazing.

That weekend turned out to be so fun. I had incredible experiences and met so many new friends. I also received a couple of new clients. Everyone was also very interested in my tarot decks, and a few people made purchases on the spot after meeting me. I laughed a lot at the event. Actually, my group was the life of the party—everyone wanted to hang out with us! I also found that space with a lot of flowers, where I ended up meeting another spiritual entrepreneur. We are now very good friends and continue to support each other.

For the entire weekend, I was joyfully celebrating my life, both what had already happened and what was to come. I was able to reflect on everything I had been through and everything I accomplished. The influence of the Laughing Buddha was definitely with me that weekend, and I know that he will happily share his high-vibe energy with you too. There can always be more laughter and celebration in life, especially when we share this energy with others.

Setting Up Your Laughing Buddha Altar

Your Laughing Buddha altar is here to help you enjoy your life. It is a visual reminder to celebrate big and small wins all the time. The more energy and focus you put into activating happiness, the more you will attract into your life. Whenever you are down and need an infusion of joy, head to your Laughing Buddha altar for a magical pick-me-up.

Here are some tools related to Laughing Buddha energy that you can use to decorate your altar. These suggestions were guided by the Laughing Buddha in a meditative channeling that we performed for this book. Feel free to add tools that are familiar to you or any others we have discussed. Always remember the Laughing Buddha wants you to enjoy life, be merry, and welcome good fortune.

Laughing Buddha Crystals
Citrine
Smoky quartz
Clear quartz

Laughing Buddha Food Offerings
Rice
Vegetables
Fruits

Laughing Buddha Colors
Yellow
Brown
Green

Laughing Buddha Tarot Cards
The Fool
The Empress
The Sun

Laughing Buddha Symbols
Fan
Bag or sack
Praying beads

Create a fun ceremony to honor the Laughing Buddha daily. It can be as simple as greeting your Laughing Buddha altar every morning, lighting a candle, and speaking an intention for the day. You could also recite commands, affirmations, or mantras in front of your altar. If you have a Laughing Buddha statue, feel free to rub his belly for good fortune.

After you have finished setting up your Laughing Buddha altar, activate the altar by calling in your Laughing Buddha guide using the instructions in the next section.

Meeting Your Laughing Buddha Guide

Connecting with the Laughing Buddha might be one of the most magical medicines that you can offer yourself. The fact that you're allowed to create and choose this level of lightness and ease all the time seems simple, yet it can transform the entire trajectory of your life.

Take a moment to find your favorite cushion. Sit comfortably and feel yourself gently drifting into lightness, joy, and ease. Tune your frequency to the feeling of joy, pure and simple, just because. Allow this feeling to expand throughout your body.

Enter your meditative state by closing your eyes and focusing on your breathing. Find yourself sitting underneath the mandarin tree. You may even feel the mandarin tree lightly tickling you with its leaves. There's a sense of play and laughter that spontaneously arrives from inside of you. Both you and the mandarin tree know that something magical is about to happen.

You may begin to imagine beautiful memories from this lifetime or envision the most peaceful images that you can create in your mind. As you do so, begin to see swishes and swirls of golden light spiraling inside and outside of you. See the vortex of light moving upward as your vibration is being raised. If any gray or murky areas arise, see them being transmuted into golden light and moving out of your crown chakra.

Notice the level of sweetness and peace in your body. You may notice a smile coming to your face or simply feel like laughing for no reason at all. Sudden laughter may burst out of you as you feel how beautiful life is and is meant to be. As your vibration raises, notice the buzzing in your hands and in your body. Allow yourself to feel this fully.

Through this raising of your vibration, you are allowing yourself to become an energetic match to the Laughing Buddha. With your eyes closed, you begin to feel an energy and hear laughter in the distance. The jolliest belly laugh floats your way. When you open your eyes, you see the Laughing Buddha arrive on a cloud. He sweeps you up, placing you in his cloud, and begins to travel through the multiverse with you.

Though he says few words, you can see the softness in the Laughing Buddha's eyes, filled with love and belly laughs. Swooshes and swirls of rainbows zoom past you as he takes you toward a different version of your current Universe. Laughing Buddha is going to show you a different perspective: the truth of who you are and the reality of where you currently are in life.

Layer by layer, you begin to see your life through rose-colored glasses. You're seeing love and laughter in areas where you didn't think love or laughter were available to you. Relationship after relationship and situation after situation are shown to you to get your attention. Laughing Buddha is showing you a different angle of each. In moments you thought were difficult, he is showing you that they were actually funny, joyful, and easy from this different perspective.

With so much love and laughter, the Laughing Buddha continues to travel through time and space and show you aspects of your reality. The gifts that you have had a hard time seeing, he is bringing to the forefront. He shows you that in every moment, there is always a gift. His loud belly laughs resound in time and space. You can feel the love, laughter, and lightness of the entire situation.

Flashes of different moments and situations rush through your mind. You begin to see how everything that seemed like a challenge was actually meant to help you grow and make you stronger. It was meant to widen your perspective in life. You see the degree of ease and simplicity that was actually available for you the entire time, now that you're open and available to see it.

In every timeline and experience, you see how many light beings and guides were with you at every single moment. You see how incredibly loved and guided you were every step of the way. From here, new transmissions of wisdom, love, and light flow into your consciousness. A new awareness of life washes over you. You are beginning to see the laughter and joy in all of your life's moments. The mystery begins to unfold for you.

Laughing Buddha finally speaks. "This gift is for you. The gift of joy and ease. Know and realize that this is always available for you. Laughter and play are always a choice and a decision. I am reminding you of this, and I will always be here to remind you of this."

Back on the cloud, Laughing Buddha zooms you through the multiverse again. Laughing the entire way, he brings you back to where you were sitting. He emits an energetic transmission, initiating you into the joy of existence. He signals to you that you can meditate and connect with him at any time. He is one with you, and with a little focus and attention, you will always be able to bring him forth—just be ready for a lot of laughter.

Laughing Buddha Joyfulness Ritual

The Laughing Buddha hopes to guide you to your life purpose through dance, celebration, and bountiful laughter. When you tap into the divine energy of joy, it will amplify your magic and allow you to fully experience a divine life. Celebration is more than just gratitude for life and the blessings that you have received; it is the energy of being one with all that you are about to create as well. When you are in the spirit of celebration, you are telling the Universe that you want more of it. The physical act of honoring your accomplishments will also reaffirm that you are on the right track and there is more fortune to come, leading you to your soul's purpose. So, rub your belly and get ready to laugh, because all your wishes are about to come true!

To prep for the ritual, you will first need to connect with your Laughing Buddha guide using the meditation in the previous section of this chapter. Afterward, gather these magical tools:

Drawing, printed picture, or figurine of Laughing Buddha

Two glasses

Beverage of your choice

Uplifting music

Yellow candle

Small piece of paper

Pen

Cleanse your sacred space and Laughing Buddha altar with an herbal wand or spray and set up your magical tools for the ritual. Make sure you are in a place where you won't be disturbed for the duration of your ritual. Your ritual can be as long as you want, depending on the time you want to stay in the energy of the Laughing Buddha and the size of your candle.

1. Sit in front of your magical tools and your altar. Pour your beverage of choice into two glasses, then set them aside for now.

2. Focus on being open to receiving whatever is in alignment with your soul's purpose. On a small piece of paper, write, "I am happy, ready, and willing to receive guidance to the highest and best path for my divine purpose." Set this intention aside with your two glasses.

3. Next, light your yellow candle while saying the intention out loud and imagining yourself celebrating an amazing life. What is the visual you need to see? What will you be doing? What will you be saying? What will be happening at that time? Make sure you embody the version of yourself who has already received this magic. The most important part of this process is feeling as if you are already living a joyful life—really lock that into your body.

4. Take the paper with your intention on it and stand up. Turn up some music and start dancing. Celebrate being on your divine path and feeling like you did in your vision. When you feel filled with joy, rip up your intention paper and say "And so it is" as you throw it into the air like confetti.

5. Come back to your altar and pick up the left glass. Toast to the Laughing Buddha's glass on the right and say cheers. Give thanks for the magic that you are calling in and then drink up! Leave the Laughing Buddha's glass on your altar

for three nights. Then, you can toss the contents of the glass into your yard. You can then wash the glass and reuse it.

6. Your ritual is finished when the candle burns out completely. Do not leave it unattended, and make sure you are aware of it at all times. If you have to leave the room before the candle burns completely, you can snuff it out with your fingers or a snuffer. When you relight the candle, say your intention again to add more magic to the ritual.

7. When the ritual is complete, you can dispose of the pieces of intention paper that you threw, or collect them and keep them on your altar after the ritual. Throw away any leftover wax. Finally, stay open to whatever messages, people, or opportunities come your way. You've taken the next step toward living in alignment with your soul's purpose, and joy is on its way to you.

Sacred Code Activations

In those moments when life feels rigid and serious and you're having a hard time finding the light and the lightness in things, this is the perfect time to tap into the Laughing Buddha Commandment.

The Laughing Buddha has a way of opening your eyes and expanding your mind so that new solutions can arrive in your consciousness. The Universe is fast, blissful, and efficient in its magical solutions that want to flow your way. When you close off your energy fields, you can create too much rigidity and seriousness in your mindset and in your body. Laughing Buddha will bring light and ease to the situation.

Another amazing time to tap into this energy field is when you're already in the energy of gratitude and celebration and you're ready to amplify this. Laughing Buddha will be here with you to pave the way to the future. Magic and bliss await you, and connecting with the Laughing Buddha is a wonderful way to speed up the energetics of this process. Feel your mind, body, and spirit rise in energy as you continue to work with this commandment.

Laughing Buddha Commandment

"Joyous Laughing Buddha, as a direct expression of the Divine, I ask that you increase my capacity to see with joy, ease, and wisdom. Show me areas where there is bliss and joy that I may not be able to see or feel. Guide me to see the bigger picture in all of these experiences, both from my past and in my future. Show me the ease, playfulness, and lightness in every single situation. Allow me to have the strength to find trust and joy in each moment. Teach me what it looks like to create a life of ease. Show me what manifesting ease in my life looks like and feels like. Teach me to relax in the moments in which I may have been choosing rigidity or hardness. Guide me back to ease. Thank you, thank you, thank you."

Laughing Buddha Mantras

Mantras are powerful activations for your energy field. You'll notice that when you say certain words, it allows you to feel a special kind of power. These words and mantras activate a unique kind of energy inside of your body. Joy is one of the highest frequencies, so when you'd like to turn a situation around, come back to the frequency of joy and play with these mantras. Mantras are best used when you are walking, jogging, or cleaning so that the words can really trickle into the cells of your body. Play with these mantras often and notice what shifts and changes happen in your world.

- In every situation, I have the ability to feel and find joy.
- When I take time to slow down, I get to enjoy myself more.
- There is always time for me to decide to fill a task with more lightness and joy.
- Love and laughter are available for me in every given moment.
- I get to decide to laugh more and allow more goodness into my life.
- There is a magic in my laughter that brings lightness, energy, and joy to all those around me.
- Laughter is medicine for my whole body.
- The state of joy brings magic, and I am allowed to be full of joy whenever I choose to be.

Laughing Buddha Ascension Prompts

When we change the way we see the world, the world changes what it reflects back to us. This is how Laughing Buddha masters reality. Laughing Buddha knows the tucked-away bliss and joy of all of life and creation. These ascension prompts invite you to step away from your current worldview and take on the perspective of the Laughing Buddha. Let the Laughing Buddha remind you of the joy, happiness, and pleasure that is already available for you. As you choose to tap into this frequency, you'll begin to see things shifting in your world; this may start with simply feeling better in your body and in your mind. Enjoy these prompts and come back to them often, because you'll answer them differently as you continue on your evolutionary journey.

1. Knowing that life is meant to be playful and joyful, how can you look at the stories of your life differently? What if you were to find joy in all of your experiences, even the ones that seemed so dark and serious?

2. If you knew that joy was an essential ingredient to ascension, what would you decide to make joyful in your life right now?

3. Make a list of all of the little things that bring you joy and bring you into the flow state. We reach a flow state in those moments when we lose track of time and it feels like everything in the Universe is just happening for us. Now, how can you do things that bring you into a flow state throughout the week? What are things you can do to uplift your spirits, and how can you choose to do those things more often?

4. If you knew that joy was the fastest way to access your guides, how would you allow yourself to create an environment of joy?

Channeled Message from the Laughing Buddha

"In every infinitesimal moment, there is room for joy. It is about allowing and knowing that the Universe wants this bliss for you as much as you want it for yourself. Allow it in and simply let it be."

—LAUGHING BUDDHA

Part Four
Modern
Magic

Chapter Nine
The Lunisolar Zodiac

The master leads you to the door. The rest is up to you.
—Chinese Proverb

Have you heard of the lunisolar zodiac? The lunisolar zodiac has recently become very popular in the West, with more and more people able to access information online. You might be more familiar with the term *Chinese zodiac.* What we share in this chapter is based on what we grew up learning via Chinese culture, but since this system is used in other regions of East and Southeast Asia as well, the proper term would be *lunisolar zodiac*.

The lunisolar zodiac has twelve zodiac cycles that interpret messages from the stars, much like Western astrology. However, in Western astrology the sun changes zodiac signs every month, whereas the lunisolar zodiac changes every year. Each lunisolar zodiac year is represented by an animal. For example, 1984 was the Year of the Rat. The lunisolar zodiac is also called *Shengxiao*, which means "born resembling." In this case, it refers to resembling a specific animal.

The twelve lunisolar zodiac animals, in order, are: Rat, Ox, Tiger, Rabbit, Dragon, Snake, Horse, Ram, Monkey, Rooster, Dog, and Pig. Each power animal adds to the unique magic of an individual's personality. In Chinese culture, it's fun to hear comments made about each person's zodiac animal. Samantha remembers her mom and grandma often mentioning that both of her aunts were born in the Year of the Pig, which is why their lives were so good and so easy.

The start of every lunisolar zodiac year is Chinese New Year, which always falls sometime around February, in accordance with the lunar calendar. (We will talk more about Chinese New Year near the end of this chapter.) There are twelve animal signs, so the lunisolar zodiac year that you were born under occurs once every twelve years. In Eastern beliefs, when it is your birth zodiac year, this is considered "bad luck." It is believed that during your birth year, you are the astrological star sign opposite the planet Jupiter. This star is known as *Tai Sui*, the God of Age, and the Heavenly General. Opposing Tai Sui in any way will bring on his displeasure.[9]

---

9. Beijing Foreign Language Press, *Chinese Auspicious Culture*, 87.

Tai Sui is an auspicious figure in Chinese culture; he helps the Jade Emperor govern the land. Because of his importance, many lunisolar zodiac followers pay special attention to every twelfth year of their lives. It is interesting to note that in Western astrology, every twelve years is considered a year of abundance and good luck, the reason being that the planet of Jupiter, a transiting planet in your natal chart, takes twelve years to return to the same sign and degree as it was when you were born.[10] Western astrologists say that when Jupiter returns to the same position it was in at your birth, it brings good luck because Jupiter is the planet of expansion and abundance.

Because we are familiar with the lunisolar zodiac and Western astrology, we understand both belief systems' teachings on the twelfth year. Personally, we think that very important, massive shifts happen every twelve years. In this cycle, if you are not on the path of your highest purpose, you will get a nudge from the Universe to get back on track. This may seem like misfortune or bad luck, but these challenges are really meant to help us figure out a solution and create abundant opportunities so we can thrive for the next twelve years. However, if we are living life with awareness, joy, and authenticity, then every twelfth year will be a good one.

As a side note, we believe that being lucky and manifesting fortune (or misfortune) all comes down to our beliefs. What we choose to believe and focus our attention on is what will be created in our reality. This is why we both choose to believe in being super lucky during our lunisolar zodiac year. But just in case any subconscious beliefs creep in, here are some rituals you can incorporate during your lunisolar zodiac year for protection and good luck:

10. Reed, *Twist Your Fate*, 95.

- **Wearing red will drive away bad luck.** Red is one of the luckiest colors in Chinese culture. It represents prosperity, good health, happiness, and success. Have your friends and family gift you red clothing and then wear it all year long, the reason being that your loved ones have also gifted you part of their luck since you might be missing it yourself. If red is not your color, then you can wear it undercover by wearing red underwear or socks. Wearing red during your zodiac year will bring you a lot of good fortune and luck.

- **Get a light that can be on 24/7 the whole year through.** A little night-light or lamp will work; personally, we love using salt lamps for extra magic. This light is said to keep us in the light of prosperity and drive away bad luck and negative wishes.

- **Wear jade.** Jade is one of the most treasured stones in Chinese culture and is believed to bring wealth and abundance. Wearing jade throughout your zodiac year will also bring you amazing luck and ward off negative energy. You could wear jade rings, bracelets, necklaces, or earrings.

All of these are simple suggestions to manifest your best year ever, even during your lunisolar zodiac year. We both have had amazing zodiac years using these tools. All year, we wore red pairs of underwear, gifted by friends, and life-changing shifts occurred. It is interesting how something as simple as wearing red underwear also stimulates the root chakra and activates grounding and safety in our energetic field. Keep in mind that you do not have to do all of these things (or any of them, if you don't want to). Only do things that you feel called to do. Remember, anything is possible, and your beliefs and thoughts are what create good or bad luck.

Lunisolar Zodiac Animal Magic

To find out your lunisolar zodiac sign, use the following table.

Lunisolar Zodiac Sign	Years
Rat	…1948, 1960, 1972, 1984, 1996, 2008, 2020, 2032…
Ox	…1949, 1961, 1973, 1985, 1997, 2009, 2021, 2033…
Tiger	…1950, 1962, 1974, 1986, 1998, 2010, 2022, 2034…
Rabbit	…1951, 1963, 1975, 1987, 1999, 2011, 2023, 2035…
Dragon	…1952, 1964, 1976, 1988, 2000, 2012, 2024, 2036…
Snake	…1953, 1965, 1977, 1989, 2001, 2013, 2025, 2037…
Horse	…1954, 1966, 1978, 1990, 2002, 2014, 2026, 2038…
Ram	…1955, 1967, 1979, 1991, 2003, 2015, 2027, 2039…
Monkey	…1956, 1968, 1980, 1992, 2004, 2016, 2028, 2040…
Rooster	…1957, 1969, 1981, 1993, 2005, 2017, 2029, 2041…
Dog	…1958, 1970, 1982, 1994, 2006, 2018, 2030, 2042…
Pig	…1959, 1971, 1983, 1995, 2007, 2019, 2031, 2043…

Zodiac Animal Characteristics

Once you have determined your zodiac animal, you can begin to uncover how the energy of that animal archetype relates to you. In this section, you will find the general descriptions of each zodiac animal and how they interact with each other, whether as friend or foe.

Rat

Rats have rich imaginations and observe the tiniest details of the world around them. They can easily spot an opportunity and find ways to create little changes that manifest big results. They are highly intelligent, quick-witted, resourceful, and creative. As far as negative aspects, they can be excessively  fearful and worried, prone to hoarding, doubtful, and lustful. It is best practice for the Rat to have some kind of mental exercise each day.

Compatible with: Dragon, Monkey, Rat, and Ox.

Ox

The Ox is traditional and conservative in their outlook on life. They easily impress the people around them with their incredible endurance, honesty, and persistence. Because of their hardworking, methodical, and grounded nature, wealth often comes very easily to  them, as does a long and healthy life. As for negative aspects, they can be too stubborn, over-indulgent, cautious, moody, and quick to temper. When luck doesn't manifest immediately, oxen should simply be patient and trust that they will be sweetly rewarded in the future.

Compatible with: Rat, Snake, and Rooster.

Tiger

The Tiger is powerful, yet sensitive and emotional at the same time. The Tiger is capable of intense and passionate love. Tigers have a rich and colorful life. They are extremely wise and benevolent. They are confident and will go out and find their luck, even when it seems there isn't any to be found. They  are both courageous and impulsive. When it comes to negative aspects, they can be proud and aggressive. At times, the Tiger may be too territorial and possessive. A solution for Tiger can be intentionally sharing things with others or donating and make it a habit to feel good about giving.

Compatible with: Horse, Pig, and Dog.

Rabbit

The Rabbit is known to be the luckiest of the twelve zodiac animals. Calm, peaceful, elegant, and beautiful are all words that describe the Rabbit. They are also friendly, intelligent, gentle, and kind. Lucky from an early age, Rabbits  are advised to treasure their luck and continue to let it grow while cultivating more and more of it. As for negatives, they may be arrogant or fickle. It is good practice to slow down and pay attention to the little details.

Compatible with: Ram, Pig, and Dog.

Dragon

Dragons are respected and revered as the
bringers of good luck and prosperity. They
are born with a lot of power in life, and
people naturally look up to Dragons—their
energy has a strong influence on others. The
Dragon is gifted with innate courage, pow-

erful creativity, and intelligence. They can be enthusiastic and
confident in nature and are often willing to take bold risks. As
far as negative aspects, Dragons can be aggressive (sometimes
passive-aggressive), arrogant, angry, and unreceptive to even
constructive criticism. A solution for Dragons is to pause before
responding and to be mindful of what is spoken.

Compatible with: Rat, Rooster, and Monkey.

Snake

Snakes are romantic, sophisticated, eloquent,
and enthusiastic in their approach to life.
People feel relaxed and at ease around them.
Witty thinkers, they are often highly intuitive.
This intuition guides them to incredible financial
security. When Snakes stay in their body and out

of their head, they are aware of the good luck around them. In a
negative expression, they may be jealous. A solution for Snakes is
to reframe jealousy into an achievable goal by adopting this mindset: "If this is possible for that person, then it is possible for me."

Compatible with: Ox, Rooster, and Monkey.

Horse

People born in the Year of the Horse are warm-hearted, energetic, passionate, enthusiastic, lively, and active. They often treasure their independence and freedom, and space to wildly roam. High-spirited and sensual, horses are encouraged to push themselves out of their comfort zones to grow. As for their negative aspects, Horses can be uptight, quick to anger, and easily spooked, and they may talk more than they listen. A solution for Horses is to befriend those who like to listen and who will make them feel secure.

Compatible with: Tiger, Ram, and Dog.

Ram

Those born in the Year of the Ram are energetic, adventurous, dynamic, and committed. People in this year tend to be creative and artistic, and they have the strengths of independence and self-sufficiency. Rams may be shy and reserved, but they know how to stand up for themselves when the occasion arises. As far as negative aspects, Rams can be impulsive, stubborn, and controlling. A solution for Rams is to consciously check in on their relationships and ask themselves if there is an equal energy exchange.

Compatible with: Rabbit, Horse, and Pig.

Monkey

Many Chinese parents love having children in the Year of the Monkey. People born at this time are enthusiastic, self-assured, and friendly, and they have very creative and innovative spirits. Mon-  keys are considered to be royal in their status, lively, and extremely quick-witted. They love hav- ing fun and playing pranks. You'll often find a Monkey laughing and having a great time. As for negative aspects, Monkeys may jump from idea to idea and have a hard time settling down. A solution for the Monkey is to plan out their goals for the next three to five years. Then, they can use this list to decide if an idea is aligned with their desires.

Compatible with: Rat, Snake, and Dragon.

Rooster

Those born in the Year of the Rooster are independent, thoughtful, ambitious, capa- ble, and warm-hearted. Roosters are honest, bright, and highly communicative, and they are often good-looking! Many Roosters also love to sing. Roosters have great luck in business  and their careers. They are visionaries who are quick to adapt to change. As for their negative aspects, Roosters can be selfish or crave external validation. They may need validation to stay engaged and inspired. They should increase their self-respect and learn to trust themselves at a deep level.

Compatible with: Ox, Dragon, and Snake.

Dog

People born in the Year of the Dog are loyal, friendly, and reliable. Dogs are honest, considerate, understanding, patient, hard-working, and sincere. They have a tendency to be overly giving to those that are important to them. They are part of warm and friendly social circles and often bring good fortune to their friends. As far as negatives, Dogs can be  cautious, stubborn, demanding, nervous, and worried. A solution for them is to be grounded in the present moment and to find tangible evidence that they and their loved ones are safe.

Compatible with: Tiger, Rabbit, and Horse.

Pig

The Pig is often seen as one of the luckiest signs of the lunisolar zodiac. Good fortune and ease tend to go hand-in-hand with the Pig. Pigs love entertainment, relaxation, and good food. A luxurious life is the life of a Pig. The Pig is compassionate, generous, and diligent, and they can  be very focused on achieving their goals. In their negative expression, Pigs can be impatient, reckless, serious, self-focused, and sometimes over-indulgent. It is a good idea for Pigs to always keep in mind that things should be done in moderation.

Compatible with: Ram, Tiger, and Rabbit.

Zodiac Sign Lucky Friends

Each zodiac sign has a lucky companion that is connected to good fortune. They are known as a hidden or secret friend and are powerful allies to one another. These are the pairs that get along the best in the real world. When you find your lucky companion, you can boost each other's magic. Whenever you honor your zodiac animal (or when you are creating your altar), make sure to include your lucky friend too.

Together, these lucky friends will create good fortune:

Rat + Ox

Tiger + Pig

Rabbit + Dog

Dragon + Rooster

Snake + Monkey

Horse + Ram

Incompatible Zodiac Signs

Since there are compatible signs and lucky friends in the lunisolar zodiac, then the opposite must be true also. The incompatible signs of the zodiac are instances in which people just don't understand one other, so most of the time they don't get along. The way that they think and behave is the complete opposite of the other sign. However, even if one is incompatible with a certain sign, if they learn the way that person thinks and operates and truly try to understand things from the other's point of view, then they can get along splendidly. To create harmony, build a relationship from the heart and have compassion for one another.

These signs are opposite one other on the lunisolar zodiac wheel and are not the best cosmic matches:

Rat + Horse

Ox + Ram

Tiger + Monkey

Rabbit + Rooster

Dragon + Dog

Snake + Pig

The Zodiac Race

Have you ever wondered why these specific twelve animals were chosen to be the animals of the lunisolar zodiac? There are many legends about this. One legend, in particular, has been passed down from generation to generation, with many variations of the story referred to as "The Great Race." This story is told to many children, just as it was told to both of us when we were growing up. In this section, we will be sharing the version that we remember hearing from memory.

In times long ago, the emperor was in charge of creating harmony in everything under heaven. The Jade Emperor wanted the earthly realm to have a way to measure the passing of time and the seasons, so he turned to the animal kingdom for help. He decided he wanted the realm's animals to stand as powerful guardians for his people. To ensure peace for his people, he sent one of his messengers into the world to spread the news about a race, otherwise known as the Great Race. The first twelve animals to complete the race by swimming across the river and into the Heavenly Gates would be part of the lunisolar zodiac. The order in which they crossed the finish line was the ranking they would have in the zodiac. The news of this race was spread far and wide.

On the day of the Great Race, Rat stood next to Ox at the starting line. Rat was not a strong swimmer, but he was smart, so he asked the strong Ox if he could carry him across the river, and Ox agreed. Once the race began, Ox took the lead, and right before he reached the other side of the river, Rat jumped off and secured first place, with Ox taking second place.

The third animal that crossed the finish line was Tiger. She was a fast swimmer. However, she did not like water and was caught in strong currents along the way, or she would've made it to the finish line sooner.

In fourth place came Rabbit, who didn't swim across at all, but instead found floating logs and large rocks she could hop on to. She hopped quickly across the river to keep her fur clean.

Fifth place went to the benevolent Dragon, which was a surprise. The Jade Emperor asked Dragon, "Why didn't you just fly across?" Dragon shared it was because he was helping some animals and humans on the way across, and that was why he was late.

In sixth place came Snake, who some say cheated by startling the seventh-place finisher, Horse, and then slithering across the finish line. Ram confidently and quickly arrived in a raft following Horse and ended up claiming eighth place. Monkey, who had fallen behind, swiftly swung through the tree vines and leaped across the stones to ninth place. Then came Rooster, Dog, and Pig, not too far apart, signifying the end of the Great Race.

As children, we were not told why Rooster came in tenth, but after connecting to the energy of the Rooster, we believe that he was a bit cocky and took it easy because he thought he would win easily. Dog secured the eleventh spot because the water was so fun, he was playing and splashing along, which made him late. Pig took the last spot—the twelfth spot in the lunisolar zodiac—

because he saw some gourmet food along the way and decided to stop to eat it and rest before making his way to the finish line.

At the end of the race, the emperor laughed and invited all of the animals to an imperial celebration with the finest foods and wines, and he gifted each of the animals golden attire to come dressed in as a way to celebrate their success. They were officially the animals of the lunisolar zodiac and symbolized new power and strength for the people and the land. From that day forward, the lunisolar zodiac has followed the order of the animals who completed the Great Race.

As we close this section, we want to add some fun tidbits of information: why is Cat not in the lunisolar zodiac, and why do Cat and Rat not get along? On the day of the race, Cat and Rat were best friends, with both determined to win a spot in the lunisolar zodiac. Early that morning, however, Cat wanted to take a nap, so she told Rat to wake her up when it was time to go. Rat, of course, said that he would, then went along his merry way. Who knows what really happened, but Rat did not end up waking up Cat that morning, and she missed the entire race. From then on, they were no longer friends.

Setting Up Your Lunisolar Zodiac Altar

You can set up your lunisolar zodiac altar to honor your personal zodiac animal and their lucky friend, or you can set up an altar to honor the lunisolar zodiac guide for the current year. It is up to you. Regardless of how you set up your altar, honoring lunisolar zodiac guides will create a cosmic harmonization with the Universe and allow you to create miracles and synchronicities in your life. And while you can activate this altar anytime, doing so on Chinese New Year will have the most powerful results.

Whether you are honoring your personal lunisolar zodiac animal or the current year's, you can use any of the following tools as part of your altar.

Zodiac Crystals
Pyrite
Citrine
Jade

Zodiac Colors
Red
Gold

Zodiac Symbols
Chinese character writings of
    good fortune
Gold coins
Money
Red envelopes
Lanterns

Zodiac Food Offerings
Oranges or tangerines
Noodles
Fish
Dumplings

Zodiac Tarot Cards
The World
The Sun
The Chariot

Create a ceremony to honor the lunisolar zodiac guides daily. It can be as simple as greeting your zodiac altar every morning (or while working with the specific zodiac guide's energy), lighting a candle, and speaking an intention for the day. Always ask for blessings and miracles.

After you have finished setting up your lunisolar zodiac altar, activate the altar by calling in your zodiac guide using the instructions in the next section.

Meeting Your Zodiac Guide

As you become familiar with the lunisolar zodiac guides, you will have an entirely new team of animal guides to support you on your life's mission. You can call upon your zodiac guides for protection and guidance, as well as for the amplification of certain strengths they may possess. As you connect with these guides more deeply, they will teach you how to work with them. Their enchanted wisdom and sacred powers will continue to reveal themselves to you as you decide to work more closely with them in your everyday life.

Head to your favorite meditation space when you have an ample amount of alone time to fully connect to your animal zodiac guides. As you sit on a meditation cushion with your spine tall and straight, take a few deep breaths, settle in, and fully relax. Imagine yourself sitting underneath the magical and majestic mandarin tree. The light from the sun bounces off the leaves, and you see various lush green colors. A soft and gentle feeling washes over you.

You find that the meditation cushion you were sitting on has become a fluffy cloud and you are now in a beautiful, open, and spacious field. With every breath, you find yourself becoming more relaxed and the colors becoming more saturated. As you gaze up at the blue sky, Monkey appears with his golden staff. Laughing and flying in on his own cloud, he holds your hand and carries you to the Temple in the Sky.

As you soar through the sky, a golden imperial gate appears. Monkey speaks to the guard and the gate opens. You fly into the Temple in the Sky together, and there is a golden staircase with a red carpet laid out in front of you. As you look up, you notice that there are red lanterns all around you, as well as vibrantly colored decor. The entire atmosphere has an air of celebration. Looking down at your attire, you see that your clothing has become woven with gold and intricate Chinese fabric. You're dressed for a celebration with the emperor and the zodiac animals.

Monkey laughs and smiles with joy, as if he has played the very best prank on you. He guides you further into the Temple in the Sky, and as you walk closer, you feel an immense sense of warmth and of being part of a family. Monkey walks you closer to the banquet hall, and Rooster makes a joyous sound as you enter the gates. Dog comes running up to you, jumps on you, and gives you a warm embrace, while Rabbit hops by to see what all the noise is about.

Tiger pulls out your chair at the banquet table, inviting you to sit. At the table you see Ox, Dragon, and Pig all eating, laughing, and telling jokes, while Snake, Horse, Goat, and Rat are at the other table playing a game of mahjong. As they notice you approaching, everyone stops and looks at you. A huge feeling of joy and familiarity rushes into the room as all of the zodiac animals come to greet you.

One by one, each animal approaches and gives you a special gift wrapped in a red ribbon. Some of these gifts are physical; others are energetic superpowers, like increased love, confidence, faith, certainty, and courage. You can clearly see what each gift is. Your entire heart feels so filled with love as each zodiac guide takes turns whispering something sacred and special in your ear and passing you their powerful gifts.

Each zodiac animal sends you off with a warm embrace. You say goodbye to Rat, Ox, Tiger, Rabbit, Dragon, Snake, Horse, Goat, Rooster, Dog, and Pig. Monkey guides you through the banquet hall to the gates of the Temple in the Sky. Getting back on your magical cloud, Monkey flies with you, leading you back to your meditation cushion. He sends you off with a warm embrace, and you both nod, knowing that you will connect and see each other again.

Come back into your body and focus on feeling fully grounded and present in the room. Take a few moments to inhale some deep breaths, integrating the experiences you just had. The zodiac guides are ready and available to connect at any time. And once you've made the initial connection, you will be able to connect with them much faster. The more you work with them, the more they can share how to co-create and utilize your powers. Have fun, and play with the zodiac guides wisely.

Activating Abundance New Year Ritual

This New Year's ritual is specifically designed to be activated on Chinese New Year. Since this falls on a different date every year, make sure you go online to research the proper time.

To us, abundance means being rich in all areas of life, and that is what this ritual is all about. We will be helping you unlock the gifts, wisdom, and magic you will need for the upcoming year and all the success, good fortune, and health you will be bringing in. We will be calling upon the lunisolar zodiac guide of the upcoming year for their help. They will lead you to your own great achievements.

To prep for this ritual, you will need to first connect with the lunisolar zodiac guides through the mediation in the previous section of this chapter. Afterward, gather these magical tools:

Drawing, statue, or print of the upcoming year's zodiac guide

Your intention for the year (what you hope to accomplish this year, in detail)

Small piece of paper

Pen

Three oranges or tangerines

Money (any denomination)

Three incense sticks, any scent (or unscented)

Incense holder (a ceramic pot with rice can work, or anything that can hold all three incense sticks)

Cleanse your sacred space and lunisolar zodiac altar with an herbal wand or spray and set up your magical tools for the ritual. Make sure you are in a place where you won't be disturbed for the duration of your ritual. Your ritual can be as long as you want, depending on the time you want to stay in the energy of the zodiac guide and how long your incense burns.

1. Arrange your magical tools in front of your altar and call upon the upcoming year's zodiac guide. Ask them to come forth and guide you toward prosperity in the year ahead.

2. Write your intention on the piece of paper and fold it once toward you, then place three oranges in front of the zodiac guide's statue or picture. Set your folded intention paper under the middle orange.

3. Light one incense stick, hold it up to your forehead, and bow to your zodiac guide three times while stating what you are grateful for in your life right now. Then, put the incense stick in your incense holder.

4. Light your second incense stick, hold it up to your forehead, and bow to your zodiac guide three times while stating what you desire in the year ahead. Put the second stick in the incense holder.

5. Light your third incense stick, hold it up to your forehead, and bow to your zodiac guide three times while stating what gifts and wisdom you would like to be blessed with. Then, put that third stick in the incense holder.

6. Place your hands in prayer position near your heart. Bow three times to the zodiac guide while thanking them for their blessings.

7. Your ritual is finished when the three incense sticks have burned out. While they are burning, make a wish list of 111 things that you want to call in for the new year. You could also journal, writing about the success you have achieved and what has transpired as if the year has already passed and you are documenting all the blessings you received.

8. When the incense sticks are done burning, you can eat the oranges or keep them on your altar until you are ready to throw them away. You can also dry the orange peels and put them in your wallet for good luck.

9. If you desire, you can continue to light one incense stick at your altar every day as a way to continue bringing forth the energy of your intention.

Chinese New Year

Since we have mentioned Chinese New Year several times in this chapter, we wanted to include some information about this special event. This day celebrates the first day of the year in the Chinese calendar. It begins on the new moon that falls between January 21 and February 20. This is also the time that the lunisolar zodiac shifts to the next animal guide. It is a very important time in Eastern culture to set intentions for the year. Many believe that what they do (or do not do) on this date reflects upon the rest of the year. Here are some rituals and superstitions for Chinese New Year.

Do:

- Eat lucky foods, such as fish to increase prosperity, dumplings and spring rolls for wealth, oranges for fulfillment and abundance, and noodles for longevity.
- Give red envelopes filled with money to spread luck and good fortune. The money can be any amount that you desire. Usually, it is married people who give kids or single adults red envelopes.
- Light fireworks to celebrate the new year. Enjoy yourself!
- Go watch the lion or dragon dances in Chinatown or at establishments near you that celebrate this holiday. Even at casinos in Las Vegas, you will see the lion dance celebrating Chinese New Year! This performance brings abundance and good luck for the upcoming year. You can also feed the lions and dragons with money and red envelopes.
- Wear new clothing to start the year with fresh energy.

- Honor and pray to your ancestors. You can burn fake money for them, light incense, or give them sweets and food.
- Hang up red lanterns to ward off bad luck and promote the energy of good fortune.
- Carry a symbol of the upcoming year's zodiac animal with you.

Do Not:

- Eat porridge, as it is thought to bring on poverty, since that was what the less-fortunate people of the kingdom ate back in the day.
- Say unlucky words like "death."
- Sweep, or you will sweep away your money.
- Shake your leg, or you will shake the coins out of your wallet.
- Wash your hair and/or clothes, or else your good luck may get washed away.
- Kill any animals, which is seen as disrespectful to the gods in Buddhism. Even swatting a fly will cause bad luck.
- Wear black or white clothing, because they are seen as unlucky colors if worn on the New Year.
- Lend or borrow money on this day. This will lead to debt.

Sacred Code Activations

The truth is that we are never alone. Even when it feels like we are sitting in an empty room, there are magical beings and guides loving us and supporting us. Our only job is to ask for assistance.

This is the power and energy of tuning in to the Lunisolar Zodiac Commandment. All of the zodiac animal guides are already available for you now, and tapping into this commandment speeds up their ability to support you on your life journey. You're so loved here. It is the animal guides' greatest joy to see you succeed in every way. Ask for their love and support—you'll instantly feel their immense magic and power.

Lunisolar Zodiac Commandment

"Sacred animal zodiac guides, as a direct expression of the Divine, I ask that all of your powers and strengths are amplified within me so that I may be an even greater light for myself and for those around me. Teach me to energize these gifts and powers in a positive way that will bring wealth, energy, and success to myself and all those around me. Awaken within me the power to activate opulence, abundance, and spiritual and worldly successes that create positive win-win situations for all. Zodiac guides, I ask that you wrap your unique protection around me, my family, and my home to speed up my evolutionary process. Speak to me clearly through intuitive insights in ways that will activate my energetic success. Thank you for all of your loving gifts and guidance. And so it is."

Lunisolar Zodiac Mantras

When asking the Universe for multidimensional support, it is best to utilize the Lunisolar Zodiac Mantras. These words awaken and activate a kind of supernatural power in your own energy field. This is the best way to tap into a kind of hyper-synchronicity, as if the entire Universe is playing and dancing with you. By simply activating these mantras with your thoughts and your voice, you'll see energy move within you and around you. Like all the mantras in this book, these are amazing to implement while out in nature, walking around town, or running on the track. Combining movement and mantras creates a much more powerful energetic effect. Tap into these often and let the miracles unfold.

- I am powerfully protected by the lunisolar zodiac guides in multiple dimensions and aspects of life and reality.
- The zodiac guides have strengths and energies that are passed down to me, and when I tune in, I have incredible access to them.
- The streams of power, energy, genius, and brilliance that are passed down through the zodiac guides are available to me at all times—I simply have to ask.
- I consciously choose to work with my personal animal guide's strengths and weaknesses in a positive way.
- I know that every day, I am gifted with new insights and awareness from my zodiac guide about how to activate my superpowers in a playful and positive way.

Lunisolar Zodiac Ascension Prompts

When we choose to see the world through new eyes, we make different decisions, and these different decisions create new results. Take a moment to dive into the world of your lunisolar zodiac guides. Each animal has a unique gift to offer you. Whether it is your own animal guide or another guide in the lunisolar zodiac that you resonate with, each animal has something very special to pass down to you. Take time to get to know each one. These ascension prompts are designed to open your mind to the world in a new way. As you read through these questions, others may pop into your mind. We invite you to keep asking more questions if new ones arrive. Asking yourself the right questions is like turning the key to a whole new world. The animal guides are waiting and are so excited to connect with you through these prompts.

When you reflect upon the lunisolar zodiac year that you were born, what comes to mind? What are your own judgments about your animal guide? What parts of your animal guide do you resonate with?

1. In what ways can you open your heart to an even greater love of animals? What do you love about them? Where do you feel separate from them?

2. Meditating on the powers and strengths of the lunisolar zodiac guides, what strengths and power traits would you love to incorporate in your life?

3. Feeling the full protection from the lunisolar zodiac guides, how do you envision yourself stepping forward in life now that you know there are twelve animal guides beside you whenever you desire?

4. This week, identify something playful that you can do to boost the energy of your personal zodiac guide. If you were born in the Year of the Pig, perhaps this means taking time to bask in the luxuries of life. If you were born in the Year of the Dog or the Horse, perhaps you'll go for a run and see how you feel. Be creative, play, and enjoy!

5. As you play with the idea of your lunisolar zodiac guides and as you feel into their strengths, energies, skills, and personalities, what new actions are you inspired to take? For instance, when thinking of Dog, you may find yourself

going outdoors more often; when thinking of Monkey, you may find yourself wanting to go rock climbing or experimenting with movement. How are your lunisolar zodiac guides inspiring you to take new actions in your everyday life?

Channeled Message from the Lunisolar Zodiac Guides

"We are here with you to experience and to create all of the magic and mystery that the Universe has to offer. Remember that we, the animals, are an extension of you. We are not separate from you. Our powers are with you. They always have been. Ask and we will supercharge your energy field. Your protection is guaranteed."

—ZODIAC GUIDES

Chapter Ten
The Five Elements

❈

Teach a man how to fish and you feed him for a lifetime.
—CHINESE PROVERB

Your spirit came to Earth to play and to create like an art-ist. The first thing an artist has to play with are tools, such as paints and colors. Imagine the five elements like an artist's color palette to remember how to create in the world with harmony.

The five elements, also known as *wu xing*, or the five actions, are a Chinese philosophy used to describe the dynamic movement and transformation of energy that occurs in the Universe. Considered to be the fundamental building blocks of the Universe, Wood, Fire, Earth, Metal, and Water express the interactions between all things.[11] The elements are often used in Traditional Chinese Medicine, feng shui, philosophy, food, and many other areas of Asian culture. They are an incredible way to bring consciousness and balance to different areas of life. The more intentional you are with color, the food you eat, your environment, and your relationships with people and the world, the easier it is to create a balance that naturally cultivates more happiness in your life.

When observing the five elements through the lens of creation, the Wood element burns up and fuels the Fire element. Once the Fire element is burned up, it becomes the Earth element, or soil and ash. Inside of the Earth element, we find the Metal element, as in the metals, rocks, and minerals that are dug up from the earth. The Metal element can be forged to carry the Water element. The Water element waters the seeds and the plants, so it nourishes the Wood element, and the cycle continues. As we begin to play with this flow, you'll notice a pattern within yourself, and over time you can make small adjustments to optimize your energy even more.

Before we dive in, let's take a moment to explore the life force energy that animates all living things: qi. Qi is an incredibly ancient concept that explains so much. When you consider qi, you become aware of the many invisible factors that can affect the health of a physical body and the feeling of a physical envi-

---

11. Morris, *Decorating with the Five Elements of Feng Shui*, 2.

ronment. And when you tend to this life force energy in a specific way, you can enhance its strength.

We love these words by Benebell Wen in her book *The Tao of Craft*: "Qi is the life force, the breath that brings vitality. Qi is the unseen impetus behind all change, creative or destructive, whether it is initiation, continuation, transformation, or cessation."[12] When Samantha studied in Shanghai, China, her teachers mentioned that there is Earthy qi, the qi that comes from the earth. There is Celestial qi, which is qi that comes from the stars and the heavens. There is qi that comes from the food we eat that our bodies extract and use as nutrients. There even is qi that is passed down to us by our ancestors, which can explain why our personalities are a certain way.

As you learn about the five elements, you will begin to tune in to the natural flow of life and creation. You will understand the significance of rest cycles and active cycles. It's important to honor this flow every day, within your own body, to remain healthy and connected to universal energies.

There is another powerful Traditional Chinese Medicine concept that we'll be diving into together. This concept explains the energy highway that powers the human body. The pathways of light and electricity that flow through the body are called *Chinese meridians*. When these channels of energy are blocked (as in the energy is moving slowly), disease is more likely to occur. Allowing the channels to flow freely creates a vibrant and healthy energy field, which translates to healthier physical and emotional bodies.

While Samantha was studying Chinese Medicine in Shanghai, one of her teachers shared the following legend: "Long, long ago,

---

12. Wen, *The Tao of Craft*, 7.

200 · Chapter Ten

there were more evolved humans who could see the light that radiated from a person's body. Because they could see the highway of light that emanated from the body, they could see where the light was blocked, and eventually this led to the creation of acupuncture—needles could be used to unblock the channels and allow the light to flow." Of course, there's no way to verify this information, but it is a fun way to understand the theory of Chinese meridians.

Each organ and endocrine gland has its own Chinese meridian network. The Chinese meridian network includes the physical organ or the endocrine gland as well as the energy highway that runs through the body and channels through the organs or endocrine system. There are other meridians as well, but we'll be sticking to the organs and the endocrine glands in this book.

The Chinese meridians and the organs/endocrine system have stronger flows of energy at certain times of the day. Depending on where the sun and moon are located, they shift the electrical currents that run through your body. These shifts are noted in the Chinese meridian clock. We've included a picture of the Chinese meridian clock so that you can easily observe which organs and endocrine glands, as well as which elements, are being activated at specific times of the day.

Studying the Chinese meridian clock can help you become more aware of your body and how your body's energy flows. The health of the energy fields of your Chinese meridians determines the health of your physical organs or endocrine system. By improving the flow of the life force of the meridian, you can improve the health of your organs or endocrine system.

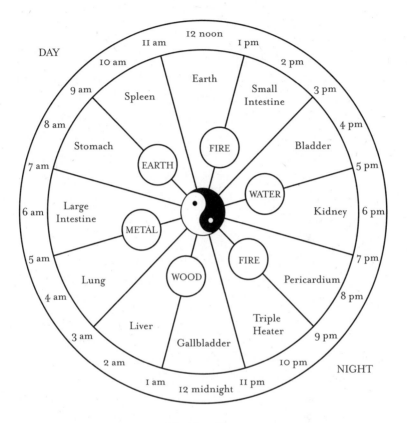

Meridan Chart

Observing the Chinese meridian clock, you can see that the Chinese meridians work intimately with the five elements. These philosophies can be extremely complex, and yet you commonly hear them brought up in everyday life in Asia. While grocery shopping in the farmer's markets in Taiwan, you'll often hear references to which foods create too much heat in the body and which foods will bring more cooling into your system. There are countless magical teas and drinks for sale to boost certain elements in your body, resulting in glowing skin, a stronger digestive system, stronger qi, or something known as blood building, which is meant to increase your red blood cell count. The average person in Taiwan has some level of awareness of the five elements, so when we were growing up, these traditions were so intermingled in the culture that they felt like an essential part of keeping our bodies strong and healthy. We still use the wisdom from these elements in our everyday lives.

As previously mentioned, there are many complex systems of *wu xing*, or the five elements. Our focus in this chapter will be on bringing joy, luck, and magic into your world using the elements. Achieving a healthy balance of all five elements can speed up good fortune because it brings us a sense of harmony and connection with the Universe. When we feel into our fortune, so to speak, we are allowing ourselves to experience an abundance of life force energy all around us. This includes the body generating and creating good energy, plenty of positive emotions, being surrounded by incredible people, and living in spaces that energize us as well as offer us deep rest. The pleasures of life come in many different forms. When we allow ourselves to expand in order to cultivate and receive all of these different forms of energy, we become a true artist, and a magnet for the wonderful things in life.

This chapter serves as a reference guide to support your understanding of the dynamic flow of energy in the Universe. Take your time as you digest these concepts. As you read, see what resonates. Then, as you are going about your everyday life, begin to observe how these elements show up for you. We recommend rereading this section in a day or so to see what new ideas spring forth. As you allow the information to sink in, you'll find yourself mastering these concepts and being able to speak about them and incorporate them effortlessly into everyday life. However, this is a lifetime contemplation, and there's always room for more fine-tuning.

The Wood Element

木

Wood fuels and powers up Fire.

The Wood element has a very powerful energy of creation. Wood is the energy of birth, growth, and expansion, and it rules the eyes, liver, muscles, tendons, and ligaments. In Traditional Chinese Medicine, the gallbladder meridian is associated with the Wood element. Wood is the energy that ignites us and gets us going. It is the energy of decision-making as well as the catalyst for all action. This element encourages us to grow in life.

On the Chinese meridian clock, the Wood element is between 11:00 p.m. and 3:00 a.m. Gallbladder meridian time is 11:00 p.m. to 1:00 a.m., which is all about decision-making and courage. When we talk about the gallbladder meridian, clients are often curious what happens if their gallbladder has been removed. I always remind them that the energy field of the gallbladder is still there even if the physical gallbladder has been removed. When the physical gallbladder has been removed, I have found that the client may feel less decisive or less courageous. I have also noticed this in some vegetarians when the gallbladder energy has been disrupted. A simple way to reboot the gallbladder meridian is to simply place your attention and awareness over the gallbladder.

Let the gallbladder meridian know that you love it and that you are aware of it. This simple act often adjusts the flow of life force to this area. I recommend doing this several times a day until you experience a shift in courage and energy. In some cases, you may want to see a practitioner to increase the life force of the area.

Liver meridian time is 1:00 a.m. to 3:00 a.m., which is for planning and organizing. In Chinese Medicine, the liver stores blood as well as our capacity to store energy, qi, and life force in the body. This determines how strong you are, how fast you can take action, and your ability to make decisions.

So, between 11:00 p.m. and 3:00 a.m., our spirit is planting the seeds of ideas, and this is why sleeping during this time is so deeply important for the body and for recovery. When we sleep, we release information back to our spirit and bring in new information as well.

Let's take a moment to reflect on the power of our eyes, which are also associated with the Wood element. Oftentimes, it is after seeing something with our own two eyes that we decide we want something different. When we think of the qualities of the Wood element and the eyes, the popular trend of creating a vision board makes a lot of sense. The eyes stimulate the Wood element in your body, which then activates your gallbladder meridian and your liver meridian to support you in taking action and making decisions more quickly and easily. You'll find that when you see something that is very pleasing to the eye, it sends a signal to your entire body to get into the mode of creation.

The Wood element is all about movement, change, and growth. Although anger often has a negative connotation to it, anger is actually a very important emotion in the process of change. You may find that when you need to make a change in your life, it's anger that reminds you of how important the decision is for you. You may find yourself in a situation that is very uncomfortable or triggering and realize your spirit has been nudging you to change a situation for quite some time. Perhaps it was anger that was the nudge you needed to make certain changes, since it is the best way to get your attention and stimulate your body's change.

Wood for Body

Green is the color to focus on when thinking of foods that nourish the Wood element. Think of all the different types of greens you can add into your diet and the fibers that will feed the microbes in your gut. A healthy gut allows you to grow more easily, both physically and spiritually. As discussed, Wood energy is all about growth. It is also associated with decision-making and serves as a catalyst for change.

This element is associated with the liver and gallbladder meridians. To support the Wood element in your body, choose foods and supplements that support the liver and gallbladder. The Wood element is expressed in muscles, tendons, and ligaments, all things associated with flexibility. In our day-to-day lives, flexibility helps us cope with change. It is helpful to take time to stretch your body each day, whenever you have a free moment during the day. When you create more space and expansive energy in your body, the Wood element can help your body change and grow.

Falling asleep before 10:30 p.m., whenever possible, is also a great way to nourish your Wood energy. The gallbladder meridian body regeneration time begins at 11:00 p.m., so falling asleep before this time allows your gallbladder to fully and deeply rest. The gallbladder is best friends with the liver, and the liver meridian body regeneration time begins at 1:00 a.m. When you fall asleep before 10:30 p.m., you allow your body to have a full cycle of deep rest that recharges your gallbladder and liver. Remember, the liver meridian is about planning and organizing. When you fall asleep earlier, your liver meridian can do some heavy lifting. Your liver meridian will support and organize your cells as well as your flow of energy the following day.

When you consistently fall asleep before 10:30 p.m., over time, you'll find that you'll most likely get angry less often, since your liver is deeply rested, and your body is more readily prepared for change. A fun tip is to also write down all of the things you want to do the following day, before you sleep, and let your liver know, so it can do some of the planning and organizing the following day for you. The liver will support the management of qi and life force energy, so that you have enough time and energy to complete your tasks.

Wood for Home and Office

Green is the color that expresses the Wood element. Take a look around your home or office space. Do you have vibrant and healthy green plants that stimulate your own growth? The green will signal to your body that it is safe to grow and safe to change. If you don't have a green thumb, you can also use green decor to stimulate growth. It is important to note that there should be a healthy balance of color in your space, so while you want the color green to be visible, you want to be mindful not to overpower your space with it, as that may be overstimulating for your body. Find the right amount of green, one that allows you to feel peaceful and at ease.

Wood for Character

The personality traits and responses associated with the Wood element are expansion, fast decision-making, an excellent metabolism, accepting change, and easily adapting in life. One of the best ways for us to stay playful is to handle shifts and changes in life quickly and with ease. To build up Wood energy in your body, practice what it feels like to expand. What does expansion mean to you? It may be as simple as going on an extra hike this week, or complimenting the people around you. Find your own edge and stretch it—see where that takes you. When you're stretching and growing, you're exercising the Wood element in your body, allowing the Wood element to nourish you even more.

Wood for Abundance

The Wood element is the ruler of spring, which means it has to do with planting seeds. When we plant seeds and take action toward intentional, healthy growth, really incredible things blossom in our lives. Do the work, plant the seeds, and know and trust that the harvest will come. If you work in the world of business, for example, seed planting may look like making a business plan, writing a book, creating a podcast, uploading video or written content, posting on social media, or networking. When you practice planting seeds with a mindset of expansion, optimism, and love, you'll find that your actions lead to even better fruit at the harvest. Your growth, like all of creation, has seasons, including the season of planting.

The Fire Element

Fire burns Wood and creates Earth.

The Fire element is a feeling of maximum expansion. We connect to this feeling when we're passionately in love or very excited about a brand-new project. It's like when a flower is in full bloom, or that moment when business is booming and a huge influx of cash is pouring in. The Fire element is also embodied by the peak of energy in the middle of a run, and the sensation of holding something in your hands that took a lot of time and energy to create. Some events, such as weddings, for example, also reflect Fire energy, as there are many steps that have to be taken for an important moment to be a magical and fruitful experience.

The Fire element is associated with the heart and small intestines. It is such an important aspect of our lives that in the Chinese Meridian clock, we see it appear twice, both from 11:00 a.m. to 3:00 p.m. and again from 7:00 p.m. to 11:00 p.m. The initial cycle (11:00 a.m. to 1:00 p.m.) is related to the heart meridian, connected to feelings of peace, joy, and happiness. From 1:00 p.m. to 3:00 p.m., we focus on the small intestine meridian, which is paired with the heart meridian and helps us receive nourishment from the food we ingest. Between 7:00 p.m. and 9:00 p.m., we have the cycle of the pericardium meridian, where we learn to build resilience in our hearts. This is often the time of day when people sit with loved ones and share stories. Sharing stories is one way to make our hearts stronger, because we build empathy and resilience as we hear about other people's lives. The cycle related to the triple heater meridian is from 9:00 p.m. to 11:00 p.m., which is the cycle that strengthens our immune system and supports our management of stress. The triple heater meridian is a Chinese Medicine concept that describes the upper, middle, and lower *jiao*. This is the flow of life force in the upper, middle, and lower parts of the body. This is how Fire energy is carried throughout the body and explains why it is a huge factor in a healthy immune system.

The 11:00 a.m. to 3:00 p.m. Fire element cycle can be expressed by the activities that we do outside during the sunny part of the day, while the 7:00 p.m. to 11:00 p.m. cycle builds up our inner Fire element, which cultivates our passion and zest for life. Both are essential pieces of creating a strong and healthy body.

To tend to this burning fire, it's powerful to breathe quite a bit, especially when an overflowing amount of joy floods in. Feel the Fire element, then powerfully ground into the energy of it, as the next energy in the cycle is the Earth element. Grounding is a way to connect yourself to Earth, so it naturally guides you into the flow of the Earth element when you take a moment to yourself. Trust that this incredible Fire element energy will always cycle back, just as all of the elements will. Instead of chasing the feelings of excitement in the moment or feeling disappointed that the feeling will go away, pace yourself in the experience and allow yourself a soft landing. Next time, you will be able to quickly prepare yourself for more peak moments.

Just like it would be impossible to feel intense, passionate love all day long, or to feel a twenty-four-hour runner's high, the Fire element is a temporary state of being. Know that this fire fizzles out, but there are things that you can do to help build it back up again throughout the day. Little things like dancing, playing, laughing, having an amazing conversation with a close friend, going for a good run, and even eating at your favorite restaurant are all ways to fill yourself with joy and kindle the Fire element within.

Fire for Body

Moments of peak expansion occur through the Fire element. To support your body in expressing this, eat foods that are the color red. Add cherries, red apples, and strawberries to your diet. You may also want to add a little red curry or cayenne pepper to spice it up. (Of course, always make sure any foods suggested are ones you know agree with your body.)

When you are experiencing peak joy or laughter, this turns on the Fire element, so it's good practice to allow yourself to enter that state. The Fire element also thrives when you explore the world with more openness. This may include going to a new restaurant once a week, or perhaps exploring a dance club. It could also include meeting new friends. Whenever you are bravely opening yourself to the unknown, you are stretching the Fire element inside your body.

Fire for Home and Office

Take a look at your home. Notice if you have anything red displayed. While you may not want to have an excessive amount of red, since that may stimulate too much action, little splashes of red can really add energy and movement to a space. If there is an area of your home that you often forget about or don't pay much attention to, it may be nice to incorporate the color red somehow. This will bring energy, attention, and awareness to that part of

The Five Elements · 211

your home. Every time you give your energy and attention to an area of your home, you bring in more of the Fire element.

Fire for Character

The personality traits related to the Fire element include being outgoing, expansive, present, and aware. When you are fully present in the current moment, your energy is fully engaged. In those moments, you will feel safe to speak and share, and you will give generously to all those around you. As you grow and evolve, your ability to expand, be seen, be heard, receive, and give begins to increase.

To exercise the Fire element, experience what it feels like to really go all-out on a project or an exercise. Due to the intensity of the Fire element, it's very important to remember that after you exert this energy, you must rest and replenish before your next energetic peak. The Fire element is not a state that you can continuously be in. However, the more you allow yourself to reach this peak level of expansion, the more you grow. Each time you're able to open up a little bit more, expansion happens. Just remember to rest and recover after coming down from your peak state.

The Fire element is also present in those moments when your thoughts are racing, good ideas are flowing in, and your heart is pumping. While in this state, write down your ideas or share them with someone. You may even want to record yourself talking about these ideas so that you can play the recording back when you need to take action—it's always best to take action from a more grounded state. To keep yourself grounded in these intense moments, balance your energies with the Earth element. Deep breathing, meditating, walking in nature, and eating nourishing foods can all be forms of grounding. Taking fifteen to twenty minutes to stretch is another easy way to access the Earth element. There are even more suggestions on how to do this in the next section.

The Fire element may be responsible for those moments when you're simply capturing your good ideas—not quite in the building stage, but in the enjoyment phase. It's still nice to get all of your incredible ideas down on paper so that when you feel more calm and at ease, you can begin the creation process from the ground up.

Fire for Abundance

When you're in your peak Fire element state, this is when you're most attractive. Often, people who work in sales know how to leverage this very attractive Fire energy. The Fire element also is embodied in moments when income floods in; this is typically the case for people who work in sales or real estate. In these moments, it's best to breathe and ground into this new energy. You can do this by placing a large percentage of your sudden income in a savings account, which is related to the next element we will discuss, the Earth element. By grounding into the Earth element, you are creating a rooted sense of safety in the body, and you are allowing the Fire element to cycle back even more quickly next time.

The Earth Element

Earth has Metal buried within.

The dark soil of the Earth element is related to both the subconscious and conscious mind. It's the energy of our roots and depth. The soil is rich in information, as it has recorded all of history, and it is rich in nutrients. The Earth element is an old, grounded, and ancient wisdom within our bodies. When we honor the Earth element, we are restored by its life force energy. Adding root vegetables into your diet is a wonderful way to replenish the Earth element in your body.

When we look at the Chinese meridian clock, 7:00 a.m. to 11:00 a.m. is the Earth element cycle. The stomach meridian cycle is 7:00 a.m. to 9:00 a.m., and eating breakfast during this time allows your body to absorb nutrients and take in life force energy, supporting the earth element. The spleen meridian cycle is 9:00 a.m. to 11:00 a.m., which supports the lymphatic system as well as the immune system.

The Earth element also includes the physical elements of life. Your physical body, your car, your home, and all the plants and other items in your home are connected to the Earth element. When you have a lot of Earth energy in your life, you will feel grounded. It is possible to have too much Earth energy. For example, if you have a home so big you have a hard time tending to it, you may find the Earth element "burying" you in heaviness.

Earth energy also shows up in grounding patterns and routines. If you have some routines in place that are helpful, continue them. However, if you find that some of your patterns or routines are no longer as helpful, or you find yourself becoming sluggish, you may try to incorporate the Metal element to reduce some of this Earth-element heaviness.

Earth for Body

To nourish the Earth element, focus on yellow foods and root vegetables. Lemons, passion fruit, carrots, yellow bell peppers, potatoes, taro root, pumpkin, and sweet potatoes are all foods that charge up the Earth element in your body. Grounding is one of the most important things to do for your body, so eat foods that ground you and connect you to Earth.

If you feel frazzled after a dinner with friends or family, for example, that is a good time to return to grounding exercises, and to ground back into your own energy field. Any time you feel a bit off, or not in your own world, take a moment to come back to your Earth element. Spending just a few minutes sitting, breathing, and focusing all of your thoughts on yourself can be a powerful grounding exercise.

A fun way to activate the Earth element is by having a weight training routine. The stronger your physical body is, the more grounded you are. The Earth element also loves routines. The more you work out at a certain time or stick to a strength-training routine, the happier the Earth element is in your body. This could be as simple as taking a walk every morning at the same time or meditating in the evening at the same time. The key is having a routine that really makes the Earth element balanced in the body.

Another great way to ground your body is through meditation. Focusing on your physical body allows you to strengthen your life force energy. While you are meditating, take time to bring your focus to each body part and each chakra. Focusing on your physical body adds energy to it. Oftentimes, we are thinking of the past, the future, or someone or something. Bring that energy back into your body instead. When you bring all of your awareness into your actual body, you'll feel much more grounded.

When you take the time to regularly do grounding exercises, you will find that your energy field becomes stronger and more resilient. Your thoughts become clearer, and you are more connected to your own energy.

Earth for Home and Office

Grounding rituals and routines are also a wonderful way to enhance the Earth element in your home. For example, you may have a ritual when it comes to watering your plants, or a cleaning routine that fits into your schedule well. When you set systems of loving and tending to your home in place, you create grounded, Earth-element frequencies in your home. Your home knows what to expect, and this strengthens the energy of the home.

To symbolize the Earth element, make sure to have browns and yellows throughout your home. Be mindful that too much brown can make a space heavy, meaning it will be more difficult to move or take action. To balance this, add splashes of color to lighten up a space.

Earth for Character

You are expressing your Earth element qualities when others can feel how wonderful you are just by being in your presence.

People in this state resonate as sweet, nourishing, nurturing, and very grounded. You can feel that their body is filled with life force energy and goodness. It's as if you can feel the good food they eat and the good actions they take simply emanating from their bodies.

When you have healthy routines in your life, such as good eating habits, going to yoga or the gym, and including sweet and positive words in your communication, you will find that your body radiates this grounded energy to the people around you. When your Earth element is too heavy, you may feel heavy, and it may be hard to even take action. If you feel that you're developing a sedentary lifestyle, then it may be helpful to tap into the Metal element, which will be discussed in the next section. As a start, you can ask yourself the following questions: Are there any ways of thinking you can release? Are there any physical items in your home you can let go of? Oftentimes, when you begin to let go of things through the Metal element, you will notice the Earth element inside of you softening, and you will be free to do the things you love with greater ease.

Earth for Abundance

In the world of abundance, the Earth element is your savings account. Having a healthy and loving relationship with your savings account can be a deeply grounding and nourishing exercise. Instead of seeing it as a savings account, you may see it as rich soil that is nourishing the seeds of abundance that will blossom in your life.

When looking at your physical items, making sure you look at them lovingly, and tend to what you currently have with care, as this will also increase the abundance in your life. When you pay attention to, and have gratitude for, what you currently have, you set a stream of energy in motion that attracts even more. Make expressing gratitude for everything you currently have a daily practice and watch as your abundance flourishes.

The Metal Element

Metal produces Water (minerals in a stream).

The Metal element represents the powerful world of transformation, releasing, and letting go. It is the ruler of grief, the lungs, and the large intestines. It is also the ruler of the skin, which is the largest organ of the body, and which allows the body to detox and release through sweat and other pathways. Metal has the energy of dissolving, dismantling, and breaking down what no longer serves the overall system.

This is the element to tap into when you are releasing a limiting belief or letting go of a part of your identity. When you let go of old clothes, delete files or photos from your computer or phone, or decide to do a deep clean of your home, these are all expressions of the Metal element in full swing.

In the Chinese meridian clock, the Metal element rules 3:00 a.m. to 7:00 a.m. From 3:00 a.m. to 5:00 a.m., we have the cycle connected to the lung meridian, which is all about releasing and letting go through the air passages of the lungs. From 5:00 a.m. to 7:00 a.m., that same energy of releasing and letting go is reflected in the large intestine meridian. This is why early in the morning, you may wake up feeling sleepy and relaxed—the body is still going through its cycle of releasing and cleansing. This is a good time to meditate and be present with yourself; allow your body time to fully release and let go. When you deeply release what's no longer serving you each day, you're able to bring more power and energy into your life overall.

Metal for Body

White is the color to focus on when nourishing the Metal element. Think of foods like pearl barley, Yi Yi Ren (Job's tears), cauliflower, white onions, garlic, ginger, white radishes, white mushrooms, fennel, and celeriac to support the Metal element.

Allowing the body to release is such a beautiful practice. When we truly honor ourselves by letting go, we are making space for more incredible things, and people, to come into our lives. Having rituals and routines that support your body in the process of letting go can be very useful. Go through your closet once a year to let go of old clothes or cleanse your body every season; these are wonderful ways to support the process of shedding and transforming. When releasing and shedding are rituals that are part of your routine, you are effectively opening energetic doors.

Metal for Home and Office

When you activate the Metal element in your home or office space, you can feel the energy of releasing and letting go. To do this, first take a few moments to relax your mind (perhaps even meditate) and allow yourself to feel into the energy of your entire home. Are there areas in your home that are ready to be organized and decluttered? As you grow and evolve each day, you'll begin to recognize things that you used to love and use frequently that you no longer use. It's powerful to trust yourself and let go of physical items in your home that are not aligned with who you currently are, or who you see yourself becoming. When you remove items from your home, you are creating space for new beginnings.

Metal for Character

The Metal element's personality is reflected in times when you need to be strong like an ax. In those moments, you need to have hard, powerful conversations to release something that's no longer meant for you. A very matter-of-fact, practical side of you may come through to get things done, and this might happen naturally, without you needing to feel or think too much about the action at hand. Metal is a powerful personality aspect to tune in to because it will help you get the job done. When you exercise the mantra "Don't think, just act," you are tapping into the energy of the Metal element. The more you embrace this energy, the more quickly and easily your tasks and projects will be completed.

Metal for Abundance

The Metal element has a transformational aspect to it. When you spend money or fully enjoy yourself in the moment, you are activating the Metal element. When you spend money, the money transforms into something of use for you: it turns into food, an investment, or an experience. The Metal element leads to the Water element, which is a very nourishing element. When you consciously spend money, you are using the Metal element's energy in a way that fulfills you. Abundance arrives when you make choices that alchemize into added value and energy in your life. This is the power of the Metal element: taking one form of energy and transforming it into something even more incredible.

The Water Element

Water nourishes Wood (growing plants and trees).

The Water element is a magical element that nourishes and supports all things. This is why it is often associated with abundance. When we look at the consciousness of water, it is joy. This joy births, and creates, more life force energy. Have you ever noticed that anywhere there is a high level of joy, healthier and happier people are associated with it?

In the Chinese meridian clock, we find the Water element time to be between 3:00 p.m. and 7:00 p.m. From 3:00 p.m. to 5:00 p.m., we have the bladder meridian, which is the energy of control and release. Knowing when to conserve your energy is just as important as knowing when to release your energy. Having a healthy understanding of controlling and guiding your energy can support you in creating a life you love, because you can direct and focus your energy on the projects that are truly enriching. Between 5:00 p.m. and 7:00 p.m., we have the kidney meridian. The kidney meridian is an ancestral energy, and it stores all vital essences. Nourishing your bladder meridian and kidney meridian supports the Water element in your body.

Water for the Body

Black is the color to focus on when thinking of foods to super-charge the Water element in your body. Explore foods like black-berries, black olives, black beans, black sesame seeds or black sesame powder drinks, chia seeds, black rice, and dark purple grapes. Most of the human body is made up of water, so the Water element is key to a healthy and strong body. By eating foods that are black, such as black beans and black sesame powder, you are boosting your kidney energy and replenishing the Water element in your body.

Deep meditation, Yin Yoga, stillness, and incredible rest are other wonderful ways to cultivate the Water element. This element is about maximum contraction, which occurs when you dive so deeply into yourself that you access empty space. You may experience a floating sensation, as if your body has completely turned to water and connected to the oneness of all creation. In these moments when you completely let go, you are allowing your consciousness to reorganize itself. This fluidity and flexibility allows the Water element to fill your body and improves circulation. Good circulation allows more life force to flow through your body, which increases the joy, luck, and magic in your life.

Water for Home and Office

A wonderful way to observe the Water element in your home is to pay attention to how the house flows. Does it feel like the spaces and hallways are open enough that energy can flow freely? Is there anything obstructing the home? If there's an area that is difficult to walk through, perhaps because of clutter or too many plants, you may want to take time to open that pathway.

The color blue is associated with the Water element. Look around your home and see if there are areas that would benefit from adding a calming shade of blue. You may also find that adding a small water fountain greatly improves the sense of tranquility in your home. However, there should never be stagnant water anywhere in the home. Examples would be a vase with sitting water, a plant that is over-watered, or a murky pond in the backyard. Anywhere water is not moving is not a healthy sign. Healthy and happy water is circulating and flowing! Always make sure that the water in your home has movement. If you have water in a vase, for example, be sure to change the water often.

Moving furniture around is another way to activate the Water element. These shifts reenergize the flow in your home. When you deeply desire a change, moving furniture around is one way to create a shift in your life while also connecting to the nourishing Water element.

Water for Character

The personality of the Water element is best characterized by an ability to go with the flow. Water can change form and move from stream to river to ocean, so when you welcome change, you are tapping into the Water element aspects of yourself. When you exercise the muscle of flexibility, trusting and going with the flow, you activate the Water energy within. This allows you to see how mutable your personality can truly be. You'll find that as you continue to embrace your surroundings, joy will naturally wash over your body. In those moments, you are in the flow of life and creation.

Water for Abundance

The Water element brings life everywhere it flows. This is why the Water element is the ruler of abundance. Where there is water, there are lush plants and colorful, nutrient-dense vegetation.

The Water element is also the ruler of sensuality and sexuality. When you are confident and expressive, it is the Water element's energy of sexuality and reproduction that you are connecting with, which births abundance in your life. Water energy is a deep inner trust which allows you to co-create your life, and as you tend to your life force energy, abundance will naturally find its way to you.

The Five Elements and Expansion

You are an ever-evolving and always-expanding human being. When you incorporate the five elements in your everyday life, you'll find that things become more colorful and full of joy. When you add all five elemental colors into your food (red, green, yellow, black, and white), meals begin to feel more fun and playful, and as an added bonus, they are incredibly nourishing. As you experiment with expressing all five elemental characteristics, you'll grow into an even greater version of yourself. As you utilize the five elements in your home and office space, these areas will begin to feel happier, safer, and cozier.

Above all else, allow your intuition to guide you as you move through the world of the five elements. Remember, this is a lifetime contemplation and journey of expansion, and the information shared here is meant to be a reference guide you can return to until you have memorized the concepts. An even fuller and more beautiful world awaits you once you have implemented the five elements in your everyday life.

Chapter Eleven
Crystal Feng Shui

❋

Better a diamond with a flaw than a pebble without.
—CHINESE PROVERB

The people of the Far East have utilized the power of feng shui for many generations. Feng shui is an ancient methodology that was developed over three thousand years ago in China. Literally, *feng* translates as "wind" and *shui* means "water." In Chinese culture, wind and water are both associated with good health, so the term *feng shui* came to represent good fortune. While this Chinese concept has been around for millennia, feng shui has really taken off in the West as well, starting in the 1970s, with interest growing over time. Many Asian Americans and Americans alike have heard of feng shui. In the reality TV series *Bling Empire*, which focuses on East and Southeast Asian Americans, they even talk about feng shui on the show.

The goal of using feng shui is to have your environment flow with good qi energy by placing certain items in specific places. When Pamela was growing up, a "famous" Taiwanese feng shui master (at least, that is what family members called him) would come and feng shui her family's home every so often. Her family said they needed to have the energy of the house flow and be balanced to bring in good fortune.

The Bagua Map

As shared in the previous chapter, according to the Chinese, the five elements are water, wood, metal, earth, and fire. Together, these elements create balance. Thus, all five are used in the Bagua Map. A Bagua Map is a diagram that breaks down sections of a space. It is an essential part of feng shui. You can use this map for one room, your whole house, or even just a table. Each section rules a specific element, and each element rules a specific energy, such as love, health, money, fame, and so on. While the Bagua Map is a perfect square, your home or space probably isn't; just match the two as best as you can.

Wealth and Prosperity Wood Purple	Fame, Fortune, and Reputation Fire Red	Love, Marriage, and Relationships Earth Red and pink
Family and Health Wood Green	Health and Well-Being Earth Yellow and earth tones	Creativity and Children Metal White, gray, and pastels
Spirituality and Knowledge Earth Blue and green	Career Water Black and dark tones	Travel and Helpful People Metal Gray

(Entrance)

When using a Bagua Map, the main entry of your home or space is always used as a way to orient yourself. (If you have two doors you use regularly, use the door where packages are left.) You will always start with the entry when mapping out your room or home, which will become your North. South is then the "Fame, Fortune, and Reputation" box, and so on. This system is similar to reading the wax in a candle spell: these directions are not which direction you are facing on Earth, but the directions of the map itself.

Feng shui is similar to astrology in the sense that you can study it for your whole life and still have more to learn—there is so much information available. Do not be discouraged if feng shui overwhelms or confuses you at first.

The Magic of Crystals

In this chapter, you will learn simple ways to pair feng shui and crystal magic. This method brings a balanced flow of energy into your home or workspace. After reading this chapter, you will have all the basic guidelines and information you need to get started right away. Of course, there is always more to be learned about this subject.

Playing with crystals is a fun and easy way to move matter and energy in your world, and to do so with intention. Bringing crystal energy into your home may be one of the easiest ways to activate powerful energetic currents and to manifest a flow of energy that supports you and everyone who enters your home. Crystals can be expensive, so remember that even the tiniest crystal is connected to Mother Earth, where it came from. Never underestimate a tiny crystal: it can be just as powerful, or even more powerful, than a large crystal.

In this chapter, we will be working with the following crystals: clear quartz, citrine, amethyst, rose quartz, fluorite, celestite, spirit quartz, and smoky quartz. These are common crystals, so they should be easy to find and affordably priced. With that being said, there are many other crystals shared in the Crystal Feng Shui Bagua Map that could also amplify your good fortune.

Using Crystals with Feng Shui

Have you ever thought of using crystals for magic and not just for decoration? Instead of just picking a random place for your crystals to reside, you can actually place them strategically around your sacred space. The power of feng shui and crystals can bring good vibes to any area. Together, they activate the specific energies of a home or space while also amplifying the frequencies of the crystals. The crystals help create harmony and a constant flow of pure, clear, positive energy. As a bonus, crystals are so pretty, making them gorgeous decor for any home.

Using the Crystal Feng Shui Bagua Map, you will learn where to put your crystals so that they can maximize the energy of your space while simultaneously boosting their own power. Once you've decided which kind of energy you would like to amplify in a specific area, you can consult the chart to determine which crystals or objects associated with that same energy should be placed in that space. You could even arrange your desk or amplify your altar by following this same map.

As always, listen to your intuition. If you have a feeling that a crystal would work well somewhere, but it does not coincide with your plan or the Crystal Feng Shui Bagua Map, you should trust your gut. Life is all about finding what works well for you! Plus, with your powerful intuition, there's a good chance your idea is spot-on: crystals have many meanings, and one of those magical meanings could align perfectly with where you chose to place the crystal intuitively. The Crystal Feng Shui Bagua Map is only a guide, so don't take it too seriously—when in doubt, follow your inner guidance.

Crystal Feng Shui Bagua Map

This is your magical guide to creating a positive flow of balanced energy for any space, even your desk. Just match up the room or space to this map as best as you can and then get decorating!

Wealth and Prosperity

Element/Color: Wood/Purple

Decor: Art, collectibles, vases, statues, flowers, a bowl of fruit, gold mirrors, wind chimes

Crystals: Pyrite, citrine, ruby, green aventurine, emerald

Avoid: Dying plants and piled-up bills

Fame, Fortune, and Reputation

Element/Color: Fire/Red

Decor: Awards, diplomas, trophies, triangles, candles, pictures of the sun, a fireplace

Crystals: Red aura quartz, ruby, carnelian

Avoid: Water

Love, Marriage, and Relationships

Element/Color: Earth/Red and pink

Decor (in Pairs): Candles, hearts, squares, photos of a couple, romantic stuff, roses

Crystals: Rose quartz, cobaltoan calcite, morganite

Avoid: Items that are sad, single, or lonely

Family and Health
Element/Color: Wood/Green

Decor: Family photos, plants, flowers, wood, floral paintings or prints, water

Crystals: Green fluorite, pyrite, green apophyllite

Avoid: Metal

Health and Well-Being
Element/Color: Metal/White, gray, and pastels

Decor: Bells, wind chimes, photos in metal frames, images of still water, round and oval objects

Crystals: Moonstone, angel aura quartz, opal

Avoid: Fire

Spirituality and Knowledge
Element/Color: Earth/Blue and green

Decor: Books, magazines, meditation cushions, bookshelves, plants, squares, lamps

Crystals: Celestite, selenite, amethyst

Avoid: Fire

Career
Element/Color: Water/Black and dark tones

Decor: Mirrors with dark frames, glass, water, photos of lakes or oceans, art

Crystals: Smoky quartz, black tourmaline, garnet

Avoid: Earth

Travel and Helpful People
Element/Color: Metal/Gray

Decor: Anything silver or black, filing cabinets, world maps, business cards, guardian angels, protection images

Crystals: Aquamarine, aventurine, clear quartz

Avoid: Wood

How to Practice Crystal Feng Shui

You are probably still digesting everything that you've read about this magical practice so far. If it seems confusing, don't worry. Let's break it down into some very simple steps that you can take to create a potent and enchanted space using your crystals.

Set your intention. Decide what energies you would like to call in. Also decide which space(s) you will be focusing on.

Then, set a crystal-buying budget. Use the resources in this chapter to select crystals that can help you amplify the energies you would like to call in; the Crystal Feng Shui Bagua Map has many crystals to choose from.

1. This is the fun part: go and buy your crystals! After you have brought them home, it is important to make sure you cleanse them before you start working with them. (If you already own crystals, you can choose one that is calling out to you.) One great way to cleanse crystals is by smoke-cleansing them with herbs such as lavender or rosemary. If you do not have anything to smoke-cleanse the crystals with, you could also visualize a golden light emanating from your hands and wrapping around your crystals while you infuse them with love and clear any stagnant energies.

2. Reference your Crystal Feng Shui Bagua Map and start matching the energies and crystals to your space on the map.

3. This is optional, but you can fill your specified locations with more objects than just crystals. Choose items that are associated with the specific elements assigned to these areas. For example, you could place objects that symbolize earth in the "Spirituality and Knowledge" area. In this example, you could add paintings of mountains or fields, or you could choose other decorations that are brown, beige, or taupe in color.

You have now created a new magical space with intention. Enjoy the positive flow of energy it brings to your home or workplace.

Crystal Feng Shui for Prosperity

Use crystal feng shui to call prosperity and good fortune into your home. Remember that prosperity is not just about wealth and money—it is about being abundant and fulfilled in every aspect of your life. Therefore, we wanted to share some extra crystal feng shui tips to activate your prosperity vortex and call in that magic.

To amp up the abundant flow in your life, it is essential to create an open, warm environment for your home and workspace. The first tip is to declutter by getting rid of things that are not needed so that they don't block your prosperity from coming to you. Make sure to bring in some plants for fresh air and have lots of natural light. Gold is a symbol of money, so decorate the space with lots of gold decor. To take it to the next level, create a prosperity altar in the wealth section of the room based on the Crystal Feng Shui Bagua Map. You can decorate it with individual items that resonate with the energy of prosperity, and you could even invoke deities and archetypes like the Money Frog and the Laughing Buddha. Most importantly, have the intention to be abundant, and believe that you already are!

Though we have provided many suggestions, the most essential thing is to make sure you feel good about where you are putting your crystals. Always place them with intention and awareness. Notice how each placement makes you feel or adds to the energy of the room. If a crystal doesn't look right or feel right in the room, go ahead and move it! Maybe the energy of that crystal resonates at a different frequency for you, and the significance of your crystal is something entirely different than the "mainstream" meaning. Figure out what works for you and what doesn't. Trust your intuition and gut feelings above all else.

Crystal Feng Shui for Love

We also wanted to include some extra magical tips for using Crystal Feng Shui to attract a loving partner.

First of all, surround your bedroom with pink and red crystals. Have red and pink paired items around the room, especially by your bed. For example, pair rose quartz towers or a couple of red candles together. Other ideas are to place four rose quartz around your bed, one at each corner of the bed frame, or to have a sizable pink crystal visible right as you walk into the room.

Most importantly, have your bedroom set up as if your partner is there with you. Have two nightstands and lamps, one on each side of the bed, and make sure your bed is decluttered, as if you are making room for your partner to be in bed with you. So, if you have lots of pillows or stuffed animals in your bed, you might want to put them someplace else!

These are just a few helpful tips to attract a partner or soul-mate, or even to enhance your current relationship, by amplifying the power of your crystals. There is no right or wrong way to do crystal magic. Crystals are always speaking to us, so if you do not know where to put one, take a moment to calm your mind and breathe deeply. Then, open your eyes and put the crystal in the place that you "feel" it wants to be. Notice how each placement makes you feel or adds to the energy of the room. If a crystal doesn't look right or feel right in the room, go ahead and move it! Maybe the energy of that crystal resonates at a different frequency for you, and the significance of your crystal is something entirely different than the "mainstream" meaning. Figure out what works for you and what doesn't. Trust your intuition and gut feelings above all else.

Popular Crystals for Feng Shui

As you have probably figured out by now, there are tons of crystals out there for you to choose from. Any crystal you choose is perfect for you, whether you are familiar with crystals or a newbie crystal collector. However, for those of you who like a little more guidance, we want to make your feng shui adventure as easy as possible. Here are some of the magical stones currently trending in the crystal feng shui world:

- **Clear Quartz:** Master healer, universal gem; amplification, focus, high energy
- **Citrine:** Wealth, happiness, abundance, manifestation
- **Amethyst:** Intuition, mental stimulation, creativity; prevents insomnia; psychic

- **Rose Quartz:** Love, compassion, self-confidence, contentment, passion
- **Fluorite:** Mental clarity, peace, wealth, protection; relieves anxiety; genius stone
- **Celestite:** Calmness, peace, detoxification, purification, cleansing; angel connection
- **Spirit Quartz:** Intuition, connection to higher self, motivation, healing; releases worries
- **Smoky Quartz:** Wish stone; protection, manifestation; repels negativity; grounding

The Five Elements in the Crystal Feng Shui Bagua Map

The five elements that we introduced in chapter 10 also play a big part in feng shui magic. You can explore the element that is connected to each area of the map to create a more powerful flow in your space. Each element has a place that they feel comfortable and at home in the Bagua Map as well as a space that they do not align with. When you add physical elements that correspond with areas of the map, you call in more good fortune.

In this section, we have shared what energy each element brings in, shapes that are favorable, colors to represent that element, as well as decor suggestions. There are also directions provided. Unlike the Bagua Map, these directions *do* refer to the cardinal directions of your physical location on Earth, so you may use a compass. When you place an elemental representation in one or all of its positive areas, it will invite in an abundance of positive energy. There are also negative areas, where the elemental energy will be blocked.

Earth

Energies: Stability, care, nourishment, trust, protection

Positive Areas: Northwest, northeast, southwest, southeast

Negative Areas: North, south

Shape: Square

Colors: Brown, beige, taupe

Decor: Plants, pottery, paintings of mountains, beige pillows

Metal

Energies: Calmness, peacefulness, clarity, productivity, efficiency

Positive Areas: West, northwest, north

Negative Areas: East, southeast, southwest

Shape: Circle

Colors: Gray, silver, white

Decor: Gray furniture, metal mirrors, silver frames, white furry rugs

Water

Energies: Flow, freshness, ease, abundance, purity

Positive Areas: North, east, southeast

Negative Areas: Northwest, west, southwest, south

Shape: Flowing lines

Colors: Blue, black

Decor: Mirrors, waterfalls, water fountains, blue blankets

Wood

Energies: Abundance, growth, health, fertility, prosperity

Positive Areas: East, southeast, south

Negative Areas: North, northeast, southwest

Shape: Rectangle

Colors: Green, brown

Decor: Big plants, pictures of forests, a brown desk, green rugs

Fire

Energies: Passion, love, success, ambition, creativity

Positive Areas: Northeast, south, southwest

Negative Areas: Northwest, west, southeast, east

Shape: Star or triangle

Colors: Red, orange, yellow, pink

Decor: Red vases, pink candles, orange pillows, salt lamps

Here is an example of how to combine the five elements and your Crystal Feng Shui Bagua Map. Say you are trying to amplify your love life and other relationships, which is the top-right corner of your space, as suggested by the Bagua Map. You can then put stars, triangles, red vases, pink candles, orange pillows, salt lamps, rose quartz, cobaltoan calcite, or morganite in the northeast, south, or southwest areas of that space.

Choosing the decor you want in each area of your home should be fun! If you are ever feeling uninspired, try creating something for your space yourself, go shopping, or ask your intuition to guide you.

Sacred Code Activations

Crystals are powerful allies that can speed up all of your manifestations. Due to their high-vibrational nature, it is always a good idea to add crystals around your home. In those moments when you want to magnetize or attract something extraordinary into your life, use the Crystal Feng Shui Commandment. This activation turns on the vibrational lineage of energy stored inside of the crystals. It is a powerful tool to amplify the magical energy that is already within your crystals. Come back to this commandment often to supercharge your crystals and infuse even more light into your space.

Crystal Feng Shui Commandment

"High-vibrational crystals that are the loving and direct expression of the Divine, I ask for your activating, awakening, and energizing abilities to bless my space and the spaces around me. With the love and the light that radiate from you, I ask that this energy cleanse, clear, and organize my space to return it back to its highest vibrational order. Connecting to your ancient lineage of wisdom, knowledge, and metaphysical technology, I ask that you bless my space with good luck, good fortune, and good blessings beyond my wildest imagination. May my space be harmonized with the Earth grid and the highest universal energies to allow more flow, peace, and ease throughout my entire living space. I ask that my home space, office space, and all spaces that I occupy become a living and breathing blessing for myself, the planet, and all those who connect to and touch my space. Thank you for your multidimensional blessings. I ask that my space be restored to its highest order to express its greatest expression of love for all. And so it is."

Crystal Feng Shui Mantras

Words are powerful. Thoughts are powerful. What we say to ourselves often tends to become real. When we practice saying new words and expressing new feelings, life will mirror new experiences back to us. Since many of us spend so much of our time in our homes, it can be easy to get caught in a rut of thinking old thoughts and experiencing the same thing over and over again. Using mantras can be an easy and powerful way to break patterns and to create new experiences in your home or office space. Saying new words in your home and about your home is like creating brand new spells for brand new experiences. See what happens when you tell yourself "My home is clean, clear, and organized" for thirty days. You'll find that by speaking these words, your body, mind, and spirit will find ways to make this true for you. Explore some of the following mantras and see what transformational magic occurs in your home.

- My home is a wealth magnet, and it brings the best people and the most amazing experiences into my life.
- My home is my sanctuary. It is peaceful and calming.
- I easily find the perfect place for my crystals to cultivate wealth and abundance.

- My space is a happiness generator. It radiates joy and happiness all day long.
- I organize the things in my home in a way that cultivates and creates even more abundance.

Crystal Feng Shui Ascension Prompts

Moving physical matter in your home is one of the fastest ways to create good luck, health, and wealth. Oftentimes, it is the tiniest things that have a profound impact on our energy and our mood. You'll be surprised by the changes that happen simply by feeling peaceful and calm when you see a messy room rather than feeling frustrated, disorganized, or behind. Each aspect of your home is a sacred expression of your soul. Treat your entire home like your temple. One area of your home touches the entire Universe. Love it and treat it with care and see what reflections show up in your world.

These ascension prompts are meant to inspire you to awaken to your own inner brilliance. Your soul has an inner guidance system that knows how to create more flow and good energy in your home and office space. Come back to these prompts often, at least once every three months. Each time you come back to these questions, you'll find that your soul has new answers for you.

- Pick any room or area you visit frequently, like your desk, your altar, or the living room. Remove everything from the area. What do you genuinely use in this space? If you were to decorate this area with love and intention, what would you allow back into this space? If everything felt efficient and intuitive in this space, where would objects be placed? What crystals would you place here?

- If you already had the level of wealth you desire, how would you feel in the space? What words would you say to yourself in this space? Which crystals would light up this space?

- If you already had the relationship of your dreams, what would you have in this space? Would you leave extra space in your closet? Would you have one side of the garage clean and clear? Would you have two towels hung up in the bathroom? Think of all the areas in your home where you'd imagine your partner with you. What would be different if they were already there? What thoughts would you have in this space? Which crystals would help inspire these thoughts? Where would you put crystals in this space to inspire and activate your senses?

- Stand in your kitchen or dining area. If you already had your healthiest body, what would you have in your kitchen and in your fridge? What words of encouragement would you say to yourself in the kitchen? Which crystals would light up this space?

- Go through each room of your home, including the closets and the garage. Take everything out of the area. (Take your time as you do this—you may need to do one area a month.) Then, intentionally bring items back in: only bring in items you truly want in your space and that have a positive energetic flow. Afterward, add your favorite crystals to charge up the space. See how this makes you feel. Does it change the way you think about things while you're in that area?

Channeled Message from the Crystal Collective

"'The light of the crystals sparks and inspires me. They remind me of my divine power and the light that is always available to me. As I see and touch each crystal, I am reminded that they are a portal to the cosmos. I feel love in my heart. I am calm, and I smile.' Speak this and connect to the crystalline energy of the Universe."

—THE CRYSTAL COLLECTIVE

Conclusion

✣

Our hearts are full because of this magical opportunity to share our unique Asian American magic with you. It is such an honor to have these stories and powerful gems of wisdom continuing to thrive and live through you. We loved sharing this pocket of the Universe with you underneath the mandarin tree.

It is our hope that you develop a habit of working with the energies, deities, and archetypes you have learned about and connected with in this book, working to manifest the life of your dreams on a consistent basis. The more you connect with your guides and guardians, the more synchronicities and miracles will appear in your life. Always be aware of new opportunities coming in and sudden windfalls of luck. If you have a strong feeling to do something that may not seem logical at the time, follow that path anyway. This may very well be your soul guiding you toward your purpose and is a continued activation of your inner magic.

It is our ultimate joy to revive these ancient archetypes from our Asian culture by sharing them with you. Your imagination and thoughts further activate their presence and prevalence in your life. Remember, ask and you shall receive! Working with these archetypes will bring you profound blessings and prosperity from all dimensions. However, it is important to remember that your guides are not solely responsible for bringing you abundance in love, health, family, career, spirituality, money, and more—it is *you* who does this.

You are the difference maker. It always starts with you. You choose the steps you take and how you want to show up in the world. We hope this book has helped you discover the magic within you. Everyone has magic and is able to use magic, but we have to remember that it is within us and learn how to use it. Working with magic of any kind is not a one-time "my life is now amazing" kind of deal. It is a habit we each must cultivate and build upon every single day. If you keep practicing, the act of calling in abundance will soon be second nature. Magic is a skill that is developed over time, just like working out, learning to drive, or using new technology. Eventually, practicing magic will be easy, and you will have better and better results.

While this book focused on specific deities, animal guides, and modalities from Asian culture, we hope you stay curious and learn about other Eastern cultures and types of magic as well. We hope that you will come to honor and appreciate the deities and guides that we have shared in *The Mandarin Tree* as we have.

Even the tiniest moments in life can be filled with so much magic and mystery. The intentions you set and the decisions you make are everything. The Universe will always deliver. It is up to you to decide what you want to receive. Approach the Universe with openness, trust, and a dash of surrender. Let the Universe demonstrate its love for you and shower you with unimaginable prosperity, health, love, joy, and absolutely everything you desire!

Seeing you as you are—a being of magic and wonder—we wish you the very best on your magical journey.

XO,
Samantha + Pamela

P. S. If you'd like to share your magical adventures and manifestations with us, follow us and tag us on Instagram: @samantha loveblossom and @pamelaunicorn. Also use the hashtag #themandarintree so that we can see all of your magic and cheer you on!

Acknowledgments

Deep gratitude to our editors, Elysia Gallo and Nicole Borneman, and the Llewellyn team for the guidance in creating the vision of our book. It was quite a journey!

Grateful for the endorsements from magical Asian American practitioners for this book; they also gave us amazing feedback and edits.

And a huge thank you to Benebell Wen for the beautiful foreword.

Lastly, this book is for anyone who has ever felt different and out of place. Being unique is what makes us stand out and sparkle.

—PAMELA

Incredible gratitude to the gorgeous souls who asked for these words to birth through us.

Thank you to all of our ancestors for passing down these mythical gems and energy transmissions to all of us.

To the beautiful readers, may this ignite a kind of soul fire that brings out-of-this-world miracles and magic into your Universe.

To my mother and grandmother for their fierceness in bringing me into the world.

To every soul that has ever held and elevated me, Pamela, and the entire Llewellyn team. A deep love for all of the numerous souls that lifted us up to create the miraculous moment of the presence of this book in the world. You are loved.

—SAMANTHA

References

Beijing Foreign Language Press. *Chinese Auspicious Culture*. Singapore: Asiapac Books, 2012.

Cultural-china.com. "Chinese Phoenix—Auspicious Bird Rising from Ashes." *China Daily*. Updated March 4, 2011. https://www.chinadaily.com.cn/life/2011-03/04/content_12117413.htm.

Cushman, Lily. *A Little Bit of Mantras: An Introduction to Sacred Sounds*. New York: Sterling Ethos, 2019. Kindle.

Hayes, Newton. *The Chinese Dragon (China History)*. 3rd ed. Hong Kong: Earnshaw Books, 2019.

Koo, Chaweon. *Spell Bound: A New Witch's Guide to Crafting the Future*. New York: Smith Street Books, 2022.

Morris, Tisha. *Decorating with the Five Elements of Feng Shui*. Woodbury, MN: Llewellyn Publications, 2017.

Reed, Theresa. *Twist Your Fate: Manifest Success with Astrology and Tarot*. Newburyport, MA: Weiser Books, 2022.

Shi, David. *Spirit Voices: The Mysteries and Magic of North Asian Shamanism*. Newburyport, MA: Weiser Books, 2023. Kindle.

Wen, Benebell. *The Tao of Craft: Fu Talismans and Casting Sigils in the Eastern Esoteric Tradition*. Berkeley, CA: North Atlantic Books, 2016.

To Write to the Authors

If you wish to contact the authors or would like more information about this book, please write to the authors in care of Llewellyn Worldwide Ltd. and we will forward your request. Both the authors and publisher appreciate hearing from you and learning of your enjoyment of this book and how it has helped you. Llewellyn Worldwide Ltd. cannot guarantee that every letter written to the authors can be answered, but all will be forwarded. Please write to:

Pamela Chen
Samantha Blossom
⅏ Llewellyn Worldwide
2143 Wooddale Drive
Woodbury, MN 55125-2989

Please enclose a self-addressed stamped envelope for reply,
or $1.00 to cover costs. If outside the U.S.A., enclose
an international postal reply coupon.

Many of Llewellyn's authors have websites with additional information and resources. For more information, please visit our website at http://www.llewellyn.com.